CATHERINE PRIGGS, HUGH RICHARDS, DAVID HIBBERT AND ELIZABETH CARR

SECONDARY HISTORY IN ACTION

IN ACTION SERIES

A **WALKTHRUs** PRODUCTION

Together we unlock every learner's unique potential

At Hachette Learning (formerly Hodder Education), there's one thing we're certain about. No two students learn the same way. That's why our approach to teaching begins by recognising the needs of individuals first.

Our mission is to allow every learner to fulfil their unique potential by empowering those who teach them. From our expert teaching and learning resources to our digital educational tools that make learning easier and more accessible for all, we provide solutions designed to maximise the impact of learning for every teacher, parent and student.

Aligned to our parent company, Hachette Livre, founded in 1826, we pride ourselves on being a learning solutions provider with a global footprint.

www.hachettelearning.com

Although every effort has been made to ensure that website addresses are correct at time of going to press, Hachette Learning cannot be held responsible for the content of any website mentioned in this book. It is sometimes possible to find a relocated web page by typing in the address of the home page for a website in the URL window of your browser.

Hachette UK's policy is to use papers that are natural, renewable and recyclable products and made from wood grown in well-managed forests and other controlled sources. The logging and manufacturing processes are expected to conform to the environmental regulations of the country of origin.

To order, please visit www.HachetteLearning.com or contact Customer Service at education@hachette.co.uk / +44 (0)1235 827827.

ISBN: 978 1 9152 6188 5

© Catherine Priggs, Hugh Richards, David Hibbert and Elizabeth Carr 2025

First published in 2025 by

Hachette Learning,
An Hachette UK Company
Carmelite House
50 Victoria Embankment
London EC4Y 0DZ
www.HachetteLearning.com

The authorised representative in the EEA is Hachette Ireland, 8 Castlecourt Centre, Dublin 15, D15 XTP3, Ireland (email: info@hbgi.ie)

All rights reserved. Apart from any use permitted under UK copyright law, no part of this publication may be reproduced or transmitted in any form or by any means, electronic or mechanical, including photocopying and recording, or held within any information storage and retrieval system, without permission in writing from the publisher or under licence from the Copyright Licensing Agency Limited. Further details of such licences (for reprographic reproduction) may be obtained from the Copyright Licensing Agency Limited, www.cla.co.uk

Cover illustration by Oliver Caviglioli

Typeset in the UK.

Printed in the UK.

A catalogue record for this title is available from the British Library.

MIX
Paper | Supporting responsible forestry
FSC™ C104740

For Helen Snelson

CONTENTS

Acknowledgements vii

About the authors viii

Series foreword by Tom Sherrington x

Introduction xiv

Part A Chapter A1: What is school history? 2

Chapter A2: A history of school history in England 7

Chapter A3: Structures of the discipline 13

Chapter A4: Conversations in the history subject community 28

Chapter A5: Progression in history 42

Part B Chapter B1: History curriculum planning in action 48

Chapter B2: Responding to challenges in history teaching through curriculum planning 56

Chapter B3: Curriculum design in practice 60

Chapter B4: Core and hinterland knowledge 67

Chapter B5: Connecting to other subjects 70

Part C Chapter C1: What is and isn't instructional teaching in the history classroom? 74

Chapter C2: How can students be given space to explore and make meaning? 84

Chapter C3: Example lessons 87

Chapter C4: Reading in the history classroom 105

Chapter C5: Writing 113

Part D   Chapter D1: Outcomes _____ 124

Chapter D2: Ways to assess for different purposes _____ 132

Chapter D3: Marking, grading and making judgements _____ 144

Chapter D4: Feedback loops _____ 152

Appendices _____ 157

Bibliography _____ 162

ACKNOWLEDGEMENTS

We would like to extend our heartfelt thanks to the history subject community; it is through collective effort that we are able to develop our understanding of history teaching in practice.

We are truly grateful for the professional development we have each received from our subject community. Over the years, the insights and expertise of fellow history teachers have prompted us to reflect upon and hone our practice. This sharing of practice is nurtured by subject associations, such as the Historical Association and Schools History Project, which play a vital role in the development of history educators. We would like to thank the Historical Association for permission to reproduce figures from the journal *Teaching History*.

The ongoing and vibrant discourse about how best to teach our discipline is both a hallmark of our subject community and what sustains it. We hope that in some small way this book will contribute to conversations about history education.

ABOUT THE AUTHORS

Catherine Priggs

Catherine Priggs is an education consultant who specialises in history education and whole-school leadership. She has worked as a senior leader in two schools and as director of a teaching school. Catherine has mentored for various ITT providers, led the history programme for a SCITT, and led and supported departments as a subject leader. She has contributed to *Teaching History*, and authors and edits history textbooks. She presents at conferences, delivers CPD for a range of providers, and works with major UK-based and international exam boards. Catherine is a member of the Historical Association's Secondary Committee.

Hugh Richards

Hugh Richards is head of history at an 11–18 comprehensive secondary school in York. He has a decade of experience in this role, working with a team of specialist teachers on curriculum, pedagogy and assessment. He is an honorary fellow of the Historical Association and has led many workshops, webinars and CPD programmes. He has guest lectured as part of the University of York PGCE programme. He has authored chapters and sections of various books about education and history teaching, as well as textbook chapters. Hugh has worked as a consultant with schools, academy trusts and local authorities across England. Hugh and the other authors are part of the team that established and leads the Historical Association's Subject Leader Development Programme.

David Hibbert

David Hibbert is head of humanities and assistant head for teaching and learning at The Cherwell School in Oxford and has seven years of experience as a subject lead in multiple contexts. David has contributed to *Teaching History* and has also presented at a range of events, within and beyond history education, over the last decade. He has also authored chapters and sections in books about teaching and learning in history, and has written for textbooks.

Elizabeth Carr

Elizabeth Carr is assistant principal – curriculum and subject lead – humanities at Avanti Grange Secondary School. She has more than

10 years' experience as a subject leader of history and as a mentor on the University of Cambridge History PGCE. She has published in *Teaching History* and presented at local and national conferences. Elizabeth is a managing editor of *Teaching History* and an honorary fellow of the Historical Association, and has worked with a number of schools and multi-academy trusts (MATs) to develop history teaching in both primary and secondary phases.

SERIES FOREWORD

This series of books was commissioned as a WalkThrus Production to complement two of our other series: The *Teaching Walkthrus*, Volumes 1, 2 and 3, and the *In Action* series. We believe that, together, they represent a powerful resource for teachers in schools and colleges in multiple subject settings.

The *In Action* series has proven to be very popular with busy teachers, enabling them to engage with a range of important ideas from cognitive science and from education research more generally. In each book, the authors explore the key ideas from a specific researcher, translating them into practical approaches that teachers can adopt in their practice. So far, the series includes:

- Rosenshine's Principles of Instruction
- Collins et al's Cognitive Apprenticeship
- Fiorella & Mayer's Generative Learning
- Shimamura's MARGE Model of Learning
- Sweller's Cognitive Load Theory
- Wiliam & Leahy's Five Formative Assessment Strategies
- Annie Murphy Paul's The Extended Mind
- Dunlosky's Strengthening the Student Toolbox
- Berger's An Ethic of Excellence
- Bjork & Bjork's Desirable Difficulties
- Ausubel's Meaningful Learning

Each of these books is a guide to interpreting the research in ways that can be applied in real-world classrooms. We have been delighted by the response to the series, with teachers telling us they value the brevity and clarity and the examples of theory in practice. It's so important for teachers to have a good grounding in cognitive science so that they have not only a clear model of how learning happens but also an understanding of all the potential barriers or difficulties that students experience. Bridging the gap between research and practice is a significant challenge because real-world classrooms are so much more complicated than the controlled conditions usually set up to investigate specific concepts in trials. The authors of the *In Action* books are all serving teachers or have taught in schools for many years, so their take on the theories and concepts that their books focus on is important and incredibly useful, grounded in the reality of teaching whole, complex classes.

It's by no means a comprehensive list – not yet – and we recognise that many other aspects of research would benefit from the same treatment. Books on Nuthall's Hidden Lives of Learners, Engelmann's ideas on direct instruction and Bandura's ideas on self-efficacy are all in the pipeline. We would also encourage every teacher to engage with Dan Willingham's *Why Don't Students Like School?*.

Released in parallel with the research-informed *In Action* series, our *Teaching WalkThrus* have also been popular with over 350,000 copies distributed across the three volumes. The idea of breaking ideas down into five-step visual guides, with short punchy descriptions, has proven very successful, allowing teachers to engage with a broad range of ideas in a very accessible format that informs their training, coaching or personal reflection. Significantly, *Teaching WalkThrus* were written in a style that is context free. They are generic in style so that teachers of all subjects in any setting can engage with them, transposing the ideas into their real-world contexts. The 150+ WalkThrus are organised into six main series, each of which represents an important area for professional learning:

Behaviour and relationships
- Lesson management
- Planning for good behaviour
- Positive correction
- Relationships and mindsets

Curriculum planning
- Assessment issues
- Broad design concepts
- Challenge, inclusion, diversity
- Detailed planning

Explaining and modelling
- Giving explanations and modelling
- Reading and writing

- Standards, expectations and scaffolding
- Types of explanations

Questioning and feedback
- Assessment
- Core questioning techniques
- Deeper questioning techniques
- Feedback

Practice and retrieval
- Guided to independent practice
- Reading
- Building fluency
- Retrieval practice
- Support and challenge

Mode B teaching
- Choices and creativity
- Making it real
- Oracy
- Student directed activities

With over 4000 schools having engaged with our online WalkThrus toolkit, we know that a great deal of valuable professional learning can be supported with our generic guides as a starting point. However, throughout each book we are at pains to stress the crucial need to adapt the ideas for specific circumstances. A five-step visual WalkThrus guide is not a set of rigid rules – it is a framework for thinking through an idea, deconstructing it so that teachers can then reconstruct it themselves, forming their own mental models for enacting powerful techniques in their own classrooms. That's the spirit.

Now, having explored research ideas in the *In Action* series and general pedagogical ideas in WalkThrus, we felt that the logical next step was to bring in subject-specific books in this new series, completing the third pillar of the trio: research, pedagogy, curriculum. Each book in the *In Action* subject series has been written by practising teachers who were tasked with presenting a summary of important ideas and debates from their subject to support busy teachers in their work. We have not imposed a rigid common format and our authors were encouraged to share their own perspectives with our readers. There is no definitive book on teaching science or history or maths or physical education – so these books are explicitly written with that in mind. The books represent the authors' personal perspective on how the ideas that circulate within each subject community can translate into great practice in the classroom. Once again, we invite readers to then adapt and adopt the ideas that make sense in their context.

I have to congratulate each author on their excellent work. It's daunting to summarise and capture the spirit of a subject, balancing depth of detail with sufficient breadth of coverage of content and related debates and implementation issues – all in what is meant to be a short book. If there is one thing that characterises all our books it is that they are accessible to teachers who are time poor. Each book in this series achieves that goal – they have an energy to them and a brilliant balance of rigour, steeped in experience with teaching the subject, alongside tons of examples to bring things to life.

We hope you find this book interesting and useful, adding an important dimension to your wider reading as a teacher doing the most important work there is: developing young people so that they have the knowledge, experience, confidence and wisdom they need to make sense of their world and play their part in the communities they belong to.

INTRODUCTION

History makes a distinctive contribution to young people's education. It builds their knowledge and understanding of the world and their own place in it: by exploring the world as it was, we explain the world as it is. More than this, history is a discipline in which knowledge is contested and constructed. Studying history inducts students into modes of knowing, thinking and accounting, engaging with evidence and interpretations from multiple perspectives. This prepares young people to understand and engage with a complex world.

Over the course of our careers in history classrooms across many different schools, we have discovered the joy and the challenges of planning and teaching rigorous, ambitious and exciting history to secondary school students. We have been teaching during a period when cognitive science has come to the fore and begun to influence policy and practice in teaching and learning in schools, contributing to a codification of teaching techniques.

The WalkThrus series has led the way in demonstrating to classroom teachers the underlying cognitive science which explains the effectiveness for students' learning of certain classroom approaches. We are fortunate in history to draw on another vast resource: years of theorisation, reflection and research by history teachers. This book aims to illustrate history teaching in action which is, above all, disciplinary – attending to the interweaving of substantive and disciplinary knowledge – but which is informed by the science of learning.

When setting out to write this book, we adopted a guiding principle: no theorisation without exemplification. We like to think that this approach, providing concrete particulars to anchor abstract generalisations, echoes the semantic gravity of history itself, where generalisations only stand in so far as they are supported by the particular and the concrete. We hope that this book proves useful to history teachers facing the same challenges that we face. Finding solutions to these helps us to pass on to our students a meaningful, usable understanding of the past and its interpretation in the discipline of history, through lessons which spark curiosity and imagination, and engage students in critical, analytical thinking. When that works, it is a thing of real joy.

Part A

CHAPTER A1
WHAT IS SCHOOL HISTORY?

History is a discipline: a way of knowing and making meaning, with its own established conventions. School subjects introduce students to the knowledge and ways of working in each discipline, offering them experience of seeing the world through different lenses (Ashbee, 2021). There is, however, an important distinction to be made between the academic discipline of history and history in schools.

The academic discipline of history

A useful starting point to differentiate between the two is to consider the methodologies of academic historians and the features of their work.

Ways in which an academic historian works	Features of an academic historian's work
• Historians work with material from archives. • Historians work with a range of source material, but that range differs from one historian to the next, for many reasons. • Historians create and test hypotheses to construct claims. • Historians tend to specialise in a particular topic or period. • Historians look at a topic or period in depth. • Different historians use different methodologies.	• In their work, historians ask questions about the past and of evidence. • Historians make claims (with use of evidence). • Historians counter, affirm and/or nuance the claims of other historians. • Different historians will deploy their arguments in different ways (i.e. historical form takes many shapes). • Different historians will consider the past through different lenses.

▲ Figure A1.1: Methodologies and features of an academic historian's work

Furthermore, Keith Jenkins argued that the audience plays a part in defining the academic discipline of history. For Jenkins, the purpose of academic history is shaped by the questions that people ask of history:

'What does history mean for me/us, and how can it be used or abused?' (Jenkins, 1991, pp. 31–32).

> For further discussion on the nature and purpose of the academic discipline of history see the second chapter, 'The uses of history', in John Tosh's The Pursuit of History: Aims, Methods and New Directions in the Study of History (2022).

School history

Knowledge of the ways in which historians work, the form their work takes, and their reasons for writing history helps us to distinguish between academic and school history. By recontextualising history for students, which enables its reproduction in the classroom, school history serves a different purpose and manifests itself differently from academic history.

Disciplinary history in schools

History is not the past but the study of the past. It is important that students can distinguish between the two. They need to understand how history, as a discipline, contributes a distinctive way of knowing and understanding the world. History – in and beyond schools – is *a* collection, and selection, of stories about the past, often competing and conflicting; it is not *the* story of the past.

Students should understand that the validity of a historical claim is dependent on the weight and status of evidence in support of it. They should therefore understand, including through experience, how historians use primary source material to learn about the past, and how they evaluate and synthesise that source material to produce historical arguments. In the work of the Schools Council History Project in the 1970s, a focus on students' interaction with sources, as the evidence base for history, marked a shift towards a more disciplinary approach to school history (although this had already been advocated by Keatinge in 1910).

> See chapter A2.

Nevertheless, students in school are novice historians, and school history is a reproduction of the discipline. Secondary school history students cannot fully replicate the archival research of an expert historian by constructing new historical knowledge from sources. For one, students lack a 'sufficient body of knowledge' to conduct meaningful archival research, which is just one contributor (albeit the most important) to the process by which expert historians formulate historical claims (Fordham, 2014).

Purposes of school history

The opening statement of aims in the national curriculum for history offers a rationale for school history which commands broad acceptance as a starting point for the design of a rigorous history curriculum (DfE, 2013).

Taking the national curriculum, history curriculum writers in schools, multi-academy trusts and external organisations create and curate their curricula with specific rationales in mind. Histories taught in schools are interpretations, or retellings, of the past for an audience of young people, and with an educational purpose. A school history curriculum might be informed and influenced by local or national priorities or concerns, trends in academic historical scholarship, or a desire to equip students with a particular sense of historical understanding or perspective. These rationales and purposes determine content selection and emphasis.

National curriculum for Key Stage 3 history.

See chapter A4.

The authors of the national curriculum for history in England were surely influenced by the work of history educationalists such as Peter Lee. For Lee, the purpose of school history education is historical literacy. To be historically literate, students need to understand that history is 'a way of seeing the world' (Lee, 2017). They need to acquire respect for people in the past, for standards of truth and validity in relation to the use of evidence and construction of interpretations, and 'a picture of the past that allows them to orient themselves in time' (Lee, 2017).

In his Medlicott Medal Lecture, Chris Culpin drew on Christine Counsell's assertion that history teaches us 'the meaning of human-ness' to argue that school history curricula should be about people (Culpin, 2007). He called for a 'curriculum for all' when stressing that school history should embrace and reflect Britain's multiculturalism. Culpin also suggested that school history should allow students to argue, discuss and make informed judgements (Culpin, 2007). Figure A1.2 provides a summary of Culpin's responses to the question, 'What history should we teach?'

We should teach students about power by getting them to question 'Who rules?' This would enable us to ask questions such as 'Who ruled well?' and 'What did it mean to rule well?'	We should teach students about the ordinary lives of all types of people.
We should teach students about war and conflict, and this should extend beyond a story of English or British success.	We should teach students about England and its relations with the rest of the world to highlight connections.

▲ **Figure A1.2:** A summary of Culpin's responses to the question 'What history should we teach?'

More recently, Martin Spafford argued passionately for history as a skill for living. 'Wouldn't it be great', Spafford asked, 'if history helped students to understand all aspects of their daily lives and culture, and if it helped them to understand the world around them?' (Spafford, 2023). The point of learning history should be that students are able to use historical knowledge and understanding to make sense of the world and to live better lives.

> The Schools History Project's 'Curriculum PATHS' (Principled Alternatives for Teaching History in Schools) project aims to support teachers to consider ethical principles for school history: schoolshistoryproject.co.uk/curriculumpaths.

While their definitions of the purpose and aims of school history differ in certain respects, Spafford, Lee and the authors of the 2014 national curriculum for history in England share elements of a common vision. They all emphasise the need for students to acquire both substantive historical knowledge and a disciplinary understanding of history. All three also highlight that students should develop a sense of the relationship between themselves and the past.

For substantive and disciplinary knowledge, see chapters A3 and A4. See also chapter C2.

Under the umbrella of aims in the national curriculum, history departments must choose what to prioritise and emphasise. A process of mediation must happen between the aims of the national curriculum and a department's curricular intent. Some departments may decide to move beyond the aims of the national curriculum. For example, a department might seek to teach world history by studying the interrelationships and links between certain cultures and civilisations to emphasise global connectedness. Alternatively, a department might emphasise a substantive concept that is not mentioned in the national curriculum, such as 'race'. An example of one department's curriculum objective and principles for content selection can be seen in figure A1.3.

> Our curriculum objective was that students were to locate themselves and their world within a much larger tapestry of time, in order to see the changes, continuities, patterns, diversity, interpretations and stories of the past. With one eye metaphorically on the past and one eye literally on the present, we aimed to give them an informed platform to look towards the future.
>
> **Our content-selection principles:**
>
> 1. content that enables students to critically piece together national stories
>
> 2. content that is considered resonant with individual students' personal identities, including local environments
>
> 3. content that addresses 21st-century notions of 'place' by embracing the globalised environment and allowing flexibility in order to account for developing global themes.

▲ Figure A1.3: The curriculum objective and content selection principles underpinning the curriculum designed by Will Bailey-Watson and colleagues (Bailey-Watson, 2019), with thanks to the Historical Association

Consideration should also be given to pedagogy – how a history teacher will teach the curriculum – but also to how students 'do' history in the classroom and how their understanding of history as a discipline is shaped as a result.

See also chapters A3, C2 and C3.

CHAPTER A2
A HISTORY OF SCHOOL HISTORY IN ENGLAND

In addition to understanding the nature and distinctiveness of school history, it is important for history teachers to have a sense of how school history has developed over time. A history teacher who is informed about these developments is equipped to engage with debates within the subject community and to draw on its accumulated wisdom, avoiding known problems and pitfalls. This section will provide a brief summary of selected developments that have shaped how history is taught in schools in England, as well as some of the agencies and organisations which have influenced trends and policies relating to school history. Developments in history education cannot be fully understood in isolation, since they have been shaped by wider patterns of development in the education system.

SECONDARY HISTORY IN ACTION

Development	Detail	Influence on school history
1906 Establishment of the Historical Association	The Historical Association (HA) is a registered charity and subject association that aims to 'support the teaching, learning and enjoyment of history at all levels and bring together people who share an interest in and love for the past' (Historical Association, 2023).	The HA has a longstanding tradition of supporting school history through various means, for example its journals *Teaching History* and *Primary History*, an annual conference, and professional development courses, as well as resources for students. Through these and other means, the HA nurtures and publicises continuous development in the theory and practice of history teaching. As the 'voice for school history', the HA gathers and represents the views of the history education community, shaping and responding to government policy.
1910 Maurice Keatinge publishes *Studies in the Teaching of History*	Keatinge argued that 'teachers who made extensive use of original sources, particularly documents, would be able to provide a more stimulating experience for their students and would, thereby, be better able to justify history as part of a core curriculum for older students' (McAleavy, 1998).	Despite Keatinge's approach not having widespread appeal, his arguments about how to make use of original source material in the classroom arguably marked the beginning of attempts to establish a disciplinary approach to history in secondary schools.
1972 Schools Council History Project (known as Schools History Project from 1982)	Led by David Sylvester, the Schools Council History Project (SCHP) pioneered a new approach to history education. The investigative nature and topic coverage of the SCHP course aimed to appeal to the full ability range of students and teaching was based on four underlying 'concepts': the significance and limitations of historical evidence, the balance between change and continuity, the problems of causation, and the importance of cultivating empathy' (Cannadine, 2011). SCHP, later Schools History Project (SHP), also placed emphasis on the value of thematic studies for strengthening students' chronological knowledge and understanding. Today's SHP 'campaigns for a school curriculum in which the distinctive contribution of history to the education of children and young people is recognised and developed' (SHP website, 2023). Its core principles, which have developed, are summarised on its website.	The birth of the SCHP marked a shift away from more traditional teaching methods which had taught school history as a body of substantive knowledge that students should recall. Disciplinary concepts, for example, were identified by others to enable teachers to teach the discipline as well as the substantive content of history. The SHP has also challenged existing assessment structures and continues to influence assessment in the secondary history classroom.

> See Henry Macintosh (1979) for further discussion on the problems of assessment the SCHP was trying to address/reconcile.

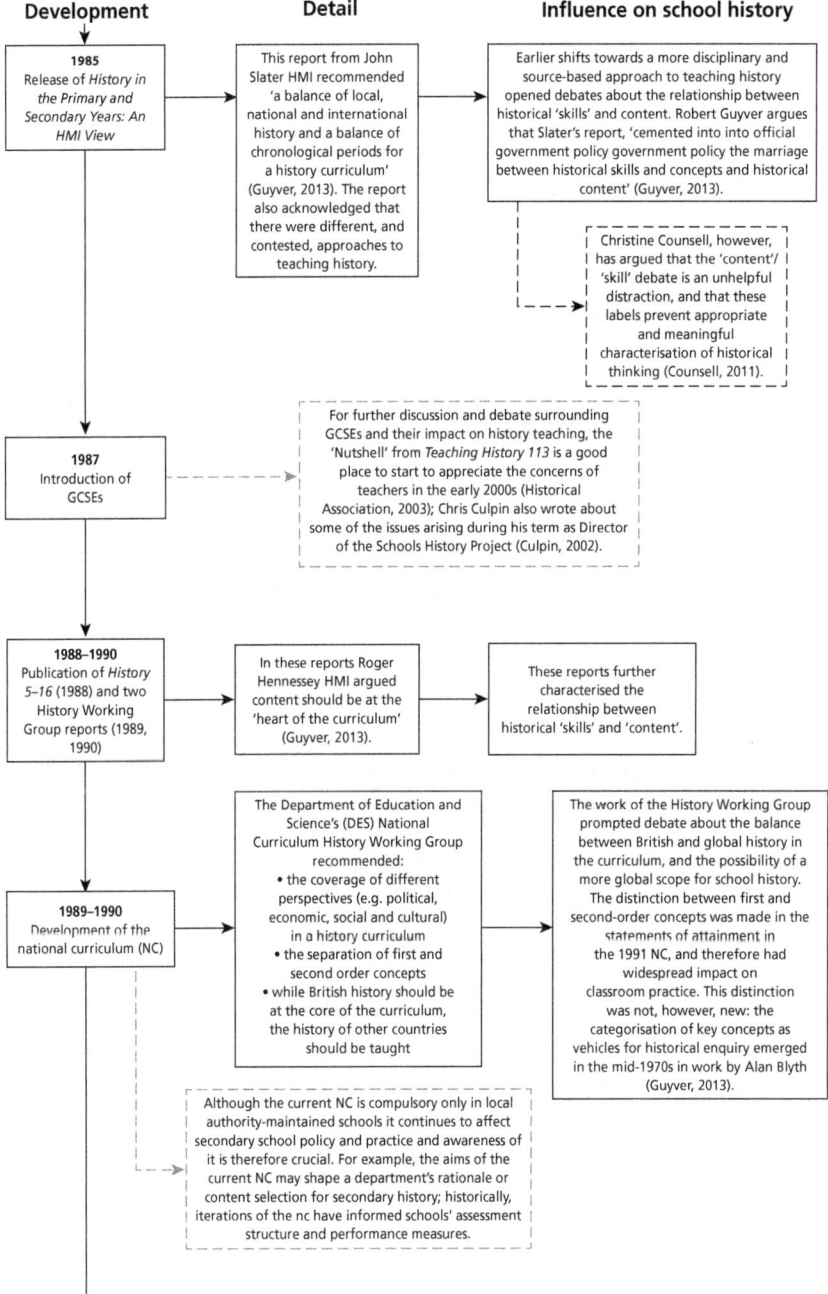

SECONDARY HISTORY IN ACTION

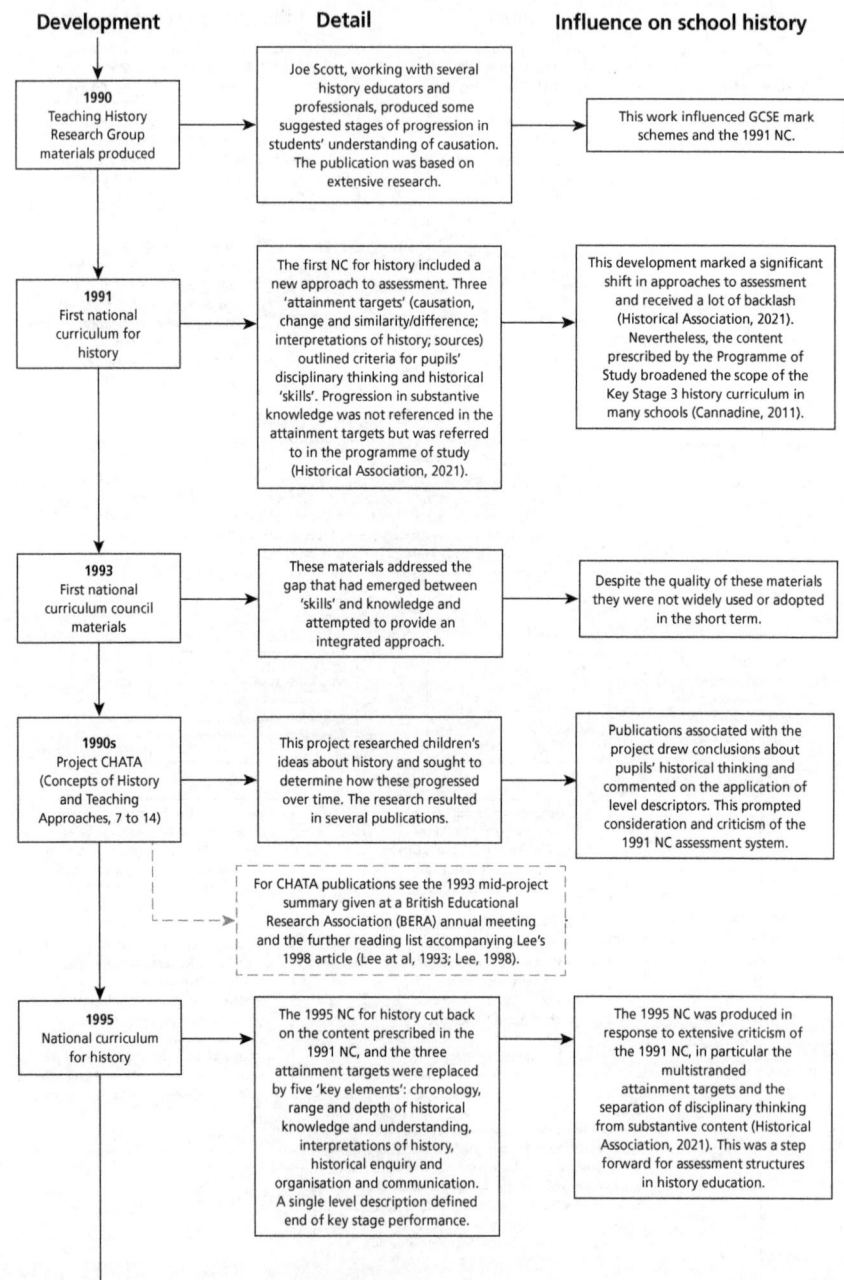

Development	Detail	Influence on school history
1998 New GCSE grade descriptors		
2007 Publication of Ofsted's *History in the balance: history in English schools*	This Ofsted report, authored by Michael Maddison HMI, found that: • students' exam performance in history (when compared to other subjects) was good, as was the quality of teaching and learning • uptake was just over 30% at GCSE, with fewer selecting history for A-level • assessment, the extent to which teaching met the needs of a range of students and allowed students to work independently, and the scope of Key Stage 3 curricula were highlighted as areas requiring attention	This report was particularly helpful for highlighting issues created by NC level descriptors. 'Part of the problem is the national curriculum level descriptions which many teachers and others find difficult to interpret and turn into workable criteria against which to assess' (Ofsted, 2007).
2008 National curriculum for history	This version of the national curriculum introduced a revised framework of concepts and processes. Students' performance in the key concepts (chronological understanding; cultural, ethnic and religious diversity; change and continuity; cause and consequence; significance; interpretation) and key processes (historical enquiry; using evidence; communicating about the past) were to be assessed against a single attainment target split into levels.	These changes were regarded as a step forward and were influenced by Peter Seixas' work on historical thinking (Guyver, 2013).
2011 Publication of Ofsted's *History for all: history in English schools*	In this report Michael Maddison HMI celebrated the quality of teaching of history in secondary schools. Maddison noted that uptake for history at GCSE and A Level had improved. He also commented that 'The view that too little British history is taught in secondary schools in England is a myth […] However, the large majority of the time was spent on English history rather than wider British history.' (Ofsted, 2011).	Maddison criticised the approaches taken by some schools including reducing Key Stage 3 to two years, and/or teaching history through a skills based or integrated approach (e.g. combined with other humanities subjects). He argued that this marginalised history and had a negative effect on pupils' performance at Key Stage 3 (Ofsted, 2011).
2014 National curriculum for history	The 2014 NC attracted much attention following the publication of a controversial draft NC. In the final version, however, the content and structure was similar to the 1991 and 1995 NCs, but with greater emphasis on the importance of substantive knowledge. Level descriptions were abolished in this version.	There was a huge response from educators and historians to the draft version of this NC published in February 2013. Concerns raised included that: • the study of history had not been extended to 16 as had been mooted • there was no connected national narrative • there was a heavy focus on English history • the content-heavy nature of the draft meant teachers might focus on substantive knowledge with little time to develop understanding of the discipline • its nature was highly prescriptive (including assigning particular topics certain key stages) The final version was very different from the draft but the discussion has helped to shape history curriculum planning in the last decade.

SECONDARY HISTORY IN ACTION

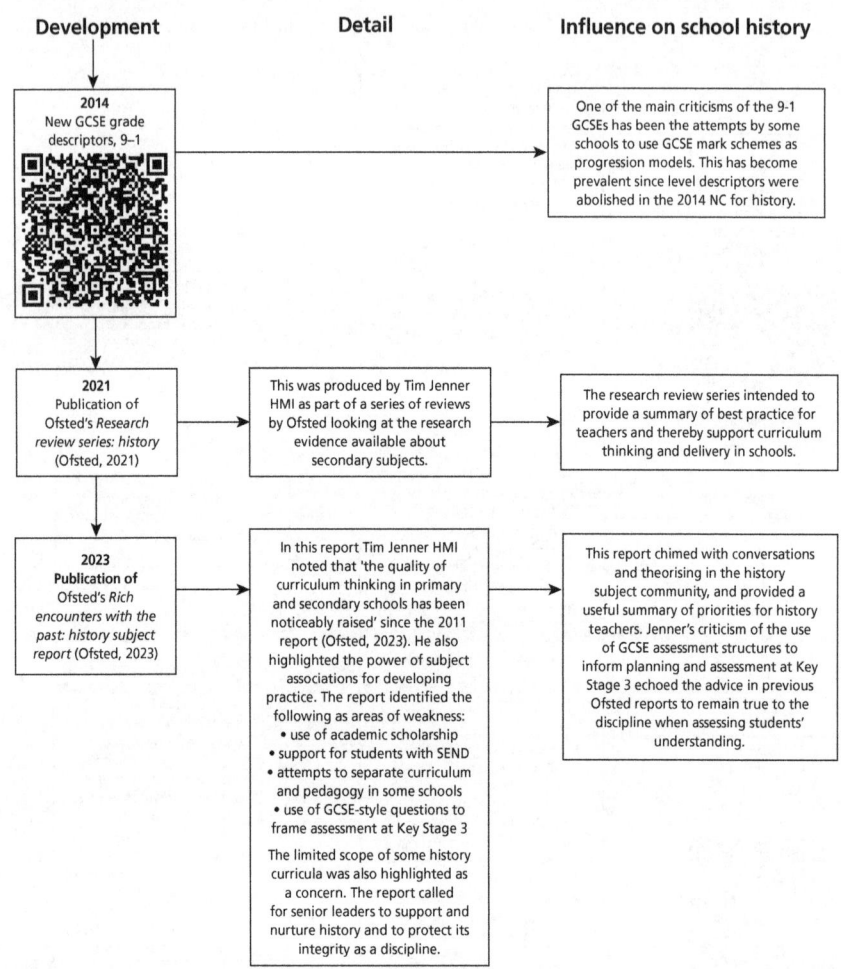

CHAPTER A3
STRUCTURES OF THE DISCIPLINE

Teaching history is complex because history itself is complex. To make sense of it, our students need three types of structures. First, they need structures to organise historical information, such as timelines and narratives. Second, they need conceptual structures to think about the past: ideas such as change, causation and significance. Third, they need a strong sense of how history is created, meaning a working knowledge of sources and interpretation. We want students to know about certain aspects in detail and to understand how a bigger picture fits together: how the tendrils of one story reach out and spiral tightly into another.

Understanding the philosophy of history as a discipline is crucial to successful history teaching. This chapter outlines two major structural threads that underpin rigorous planning and meaningful teaching of school history: knowledge about the past (substantive knowledge) and knowledge about how historians study the past (disciplinary knowledge) (Ofsted, 2021).

> Chapter A2 shows us how history teachers have addressed issues relating to school history over time.

A key feature of a rigorous history curriculum is the interplay between substantive and disciplinary knowledge. Strong history teaching will skilfully plait together both types of knowledge so that students do not interact with them in silos.

Substantive knowledge

Put simply, this is the 'stuff that happened': the events and the people caught up in them. How substantive knowledge is selected, organised and taught has a huge impact on students' ability to combine it with disciplinary concepts to answer challenging historical questions.

> **Disciplinary knowledge**
>
> Disciplinary knowledge is that which students acquire about how history works, and what historians do (Counsell, 2018b). This includes how historians identify and use sources of evidence, how they formulate historical claims, and how they support those claims with evidence. Among those conventions are the organising concepts of the discipline.

Planned interactions between substantive and disciplinary knowledge are crucial. To focus on substantive knowledge alone would impart information to students but would not teach them history. Attempts to teach disciplinary knowledge in isolation – for example, in a 'What is history?' enquiry at the start of Key Stage 3, which introduces disciplinary concepts – is equally problematical. Practical, concrete exemplification of history in practice – engaging with substantive content through a disciplinary lens – will do more to help novice learners embarking on a secondary education to understand the discipline of history than learning about the philosophy of history in the abstract. Students cannot begin to understand or appreciate the craft of a historian without a substantive focus. The necessity for this relationship is explained in Ofsted's research review for history:

> ...knowledge of the past must be shaped by disciplinary approaches in order to become historical knowledge. Similarly, acquiring disciplinary knowledge is made purposeful and meaningful to pupils when it is related to particular historical problems where pupils have sufficient knowledge of the period, setting and topic to reason, to make inferences and to grasp the terms that others are using in any debate. (Ofsted, 2021)

Communicating historical understanding requires students to deploy substantive and disciplinary knowledge in combination. If disciplinary approaches have not shaped students' study of the past, or equally, if students are unable to utilise rich and relevant substantive knowledge when presenting an historical argument, they are not engaging with history as a discipline. Imagining history without each helps us perceive the importance of combining them both, as set out in figure A3.1.

With insufficient attention to...	...we risk...
substantive knowledge	...superficial debates centred on disciplinary concepts that get no further than unsubstantiated opinion, rendering them largely meaningless. to become historical understanding, substantive knowledge must be used in connection with the disciplinary concepts.
substantive concepts	...students without the terminology and conceptual framework to break down historical situations into analytical parts, limiting their ability to build their own substantive knowledge and arrive at valid conclusions when applying disciplinary skills.
disciplinary concepts	...the past becoming a singular chronological story. aside from being far removed from the contested nature of the discipline, this has the potential to be both dull and dangerous.

▲ Figure A3.1: The importance of substantive and disciplinary knowledge

Categories of substantive knowledge

Describing substantive knowledge as the 'content' of the past is helpful for distinguishing it from disciplinary knowledge; further categorising substantive knowledge according to its function is also vital for successful history teaching.

Fingertip and residue knowledge

Christine Counsell classified the types of historical knowledge used by teachers as 'fingertip' and 'residue' knowledge (Counsell, 2011). Fingertip knowledge allows students to access topics as they are taught, but this is knowledge that can be forgotten and is not essential for future learning (see also Grande, 2022). Residue knowledge is the detail left behind from fingertip knowledge which, over time, leaves students with a broad historical understanding (Counsell, 2000).

Core and hinterland knowledge

Subsequently, Counsell used the terms 'core' and 'hinterland' to further distinguish the curricular functions of knowledge (Counsell, 2018). 'Core' content is what we aim for students

See chapter B4.

to retain – 'the things that can be captured as proposition' (Counsell, 2018). 'Hinterland' is contextual or background detail that serves the proximal function of enabling students to generate and arrive at core propositions.

Understanding the relationship between core and hinterland knowledge is essential when planning a history curriculum. Although students can forget the hinterland knowledge and still achieve the ultimate aims of the curriculum, hinterland knowledge is crucial for facilitating and enabling historical understanding. Hinterland is not an optional extra – an entertaining story told here or there to engage students. Without hinterland fostering students' sense of period and historical perspective, the core is meaningless. Jonathan Grande argues that '[t]he core is abstract without hinterland – hinterland makes meaning of knowledge' (Grande, 2022). Figure A3.2 exemplifies some ways in which history teachers have planned for hinterland knowledge in the curriculum.

Use of hinterland knowledge to demystify abstract topics/concepts	Use of hinterland knowledge to contextualise understanding of an event	Use of hinterland knowledge to prepare students for future learning
Jonathan Grande has offered rich reflections on the role of hinterland knowledge, and concrete examples of why it is important for classroom practice (Grande, 2022).	In his article on 'worldbuilding', Mike Hill reflects on his use of maps of communist insurgencies in Germany between 1919 and 1924. He argues that his students having knowledge of these uprisings was '… not strictly instrumental to the core narrative but fleshed out the world within which this narrative unfolded…' (Hill, 2020).	Ed Durbin argued that developing his students' capacity to become better analytical thinkers was greatly aided by the inclusion of hinterland knowledge throughout Key Stage 3 (Durbin, 2018).

▲ Figure A3.2: Uses of hinterland knowledge

When planning a curriculum, it is crucial to consider how students' core historical understanding will manifest, so that we are clear on the function of each part of the curriculum. See appendix 1 for one department's 'curriculum takeaways', or intention for core knowledge.

Substantive concepts

Substantive concepts are ideas to which students return in different contexts throughout their study of history. The Historical Association defines substantive concepts as 'those concerned with the subject matter of history – the substance about which students are learning', and highlight that:

- some are highly specific to period or place
- some can originate in a specific context but develop to have wider resonance and use
- some have a wide application, can be applied in many contexts, and are not history-specific.

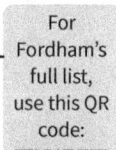

Substantive concepts: see the section guide from the Historical Association (history.org.uk).

Michael Fordham has listed many examples that might appear in a Key Stage 3 curriculum, including concepts such as class, imperialism and trade unions.

For Fordham's full list, use this QR code:

As students revisit these concepts, they should detect changes in their meanings in different historical contexts. It is therefore essential that students' encounters with substantive concepts are period- and context-specific. History teachers have planned for students' encounters with substantive concepts in their curriculum in several ways (figure A3.3).

Theme	Examples
Students' understanding of substantive concepts over time	• Dominik Palek reflected on his students' understanding of 'parliament' and their wider substantive knowledge (Palek, 2015). • Alexander Bridges gave thought to how his students' understanding of substantive concepts grew and developed over time (Bridges, 2018).
Assessment	• Sally Burnham and Geraint Brown (2014) considered how assessment can be used to probe students' understanding of substantive concepts.
Wider curriculum planning	• Elizabeth Carr (2021) discussed how her department made use of substantive concepts to underpin curriculum planning.

▲ A3.3: Planning for encounters with substantive knowledge

Substantive concepts in the history classroom

Substantive concepts are challenging for history teachers to teach and for students to understand. Considerations when planning for students to develop knowledge and understanding of substantive concepts include:

1. Substantive concepts defy simple definition.

As Fordham notes, substantive concepts are not 'vocabulary' in the traditional sense:

> Although learning a definition might be appropriate for some of these words, this alone is unlikely to be sufficient. At best, a definition might be a "leg-up" into the word, but one that will need a great deal of further elaboration. This means that these words need to be encountered multiple times throughout a curriculum, with each encounter adding another layer of meaning to the word. (Fordham, 2017a)

Concepts are hard to define. In history some concepts are additionally hard to define because they change in meaning over time. For example, any definition of 'parliament' as the term is used in a 20th century context would be dramatically different to how Simon de Montfort's 1265 'parliament' looked, which was in turn barely recognisable when compared to what Oliver Cromwell meant by 'parliament' (Palek, 2015). Not only does the term change its substantive meaning over time, but these changes are critical to students' understanding the nature of change.

Indeed, definitions can hamper understanding and require unpicking. The definition of 'knight' in the context of the Norman invasion of England in 1066 does not accurately capture the meaning of 'knight' at the Elizabethan court. Our students face other linguistic issues too:

- different words for the same thing over time (privy, toilet)
- words used in the past that mean something different today (tablet, meme)
- multiple words used for very similar things within a time period (priory, abbey) or across time periods (baron, lord, noble, earl, landowner, aristocrat).

Fordham offers a short blog which elucidates this issue:

Expert historians interpret these words correctly in context, drawing on their extensive knowledge, while novice students often do not. Teachers therefore need to plan for students to encounter these concepts multiple times, sharpening their contextual awareness. This is illustrated in relation to revolutions in figure A3.4.

2. We can emphasise selected key concepts by returning to them more often.

Frequency is important in this selection process. Students should bump into certain core substantive concepts regularly throughout a curriculum, for example class, race or revolution. They might encounter others just once or twice, in the appropriate historical context.

How often students come across a particular concept is, in practice, shaped by the selection of content in the curriculum. This is a reciprocal process, however. It is important to choose stories that illustrate a sufficiently broad range of substantive concepts.

3. We need to think carefully about how many we try to teach.

With limited curriculum time, history teachers cannot provide repeated encounters with, and do justice to, the nuanced meaning of every possible substantive concept. Inevitably, we must plan a curriculum that emphasises certain concepts over others.

The following criteria may help history teachers to select which substantive concepts to emphasise:

- concepts that are fundamental in historical discourse (class, race, society)
- concepts that are foundational to particular topics in the curriculum, and especially those which recur (communism, monarchy)
- concepts that enhance students' understanding of the world around them (democracy, propaganda).

4. When to introduce substantive concepts.

Certain concepts are particularly associated with a certain historical period or development; they may have been coined by contemporaries or historians to describe a feature of that era. These concepts are particularly powerful for unlocking students' understanding of these periods and developments. 'Ideology' is a good example. Although historians use this term in studies of political cultures across time, it may be most effective to introduce this to students studying fascism studying fascism and communism in the twentieth century. Students might first encounter this concept at Key Stage 3, and study it again in more detail at Key Stage 4. At Key Stage 5, students might be sufficiently familiar with the concept that they are ready to consider its application to other periods, for example by considering the question 'Was Renaissance humanism a political ideology?'. As a counter-example, a concept such as 'propaganda', although coined in a later period, could be introduced when studying Tudor portraiture at Key Stage 3.

A worked example: revolution

Figure A3.4 illustrates a practical example of a key substantive concept, revolution, mapped across a curriculum.

Encounters with the concept of revolution across a secondary school			
Year 7	Year 8	Year 9	GCSE & A-level
English Civil War	scientific revolution	Russian revolution	scientific revolution
	French revolution	Cuban revolution	1918–19 German revolution
	Haitian revolution	Chinese revolution	
	American revolution		John Guy's argument about a 'revolution' in Tudor government
	industrial revolution		

▲ Figure A3.4: Revolution as a key substantive concept mapped across a curriculum

Things to note about this example:

Some of these topics create opportunities for students to debate whether or not a given event 'qualifies' as a revolution. Such a debate can consolidate students' conceptual understanding through discussion of and reflection on the meaning of revolution in different contexts, and the ways in which the application of a label such as revolution conveys historical interpretation.

In this curriculum, the Year 8 course in particular provides multiple encounters with revolution as a concept. Studying the Age of Revolutions allows students to build up layers of examples, and to explore the scope and nuances of the concept.

Identifying substantive concepts and planning for how they can be layered across a curriculum plays an important role in helping students make sense of the past and how it is interpreted by historians.

Disciplinary knowledge

The importance of students understanding history as a discipline was explored in chapter A1. A history curriculum must allow students to distinguish the process of history from the substance of the past, which is its object of study. To do this, students need to know how historians investigate the past, and how they construct historical arguments and claims. This is disciplinary knowledge.

Disciplinary concepts

The development of disciplinary knowledge is among the aims outlined in the national curriculum for history, where a number of disciplinary concepts are identified.

> The term 'second-order concepts' has been used to describe the concepts historians (and students of history) use for thinking about the past. They are now commonly referred to as 'disciplinary concepts'.

Disciplinary concepts are abstractions that allow teachers and students to give shape and meaning to their study of the past and to engage in its interpretation. For example, students could study the First World War in many different ways: the changes in tactics over time, the similarity and difference in contemporary experiences or the causes behind the allied victory. The Historical Association has published a series of guides entitled 'What's the wisdom on...?' Several of these outline research and classroom practice by history teachers in relation to teaching disciplinary concepts to secondary school students. Figure A3.5 outlines important disciplinary concepts in history, with links to the relevant 'What's the wisdom on...?' article.

Disciplinary concept	Description	Link
Cause and consequence	Analyses the reasons for events, processes or developments and/or their results. For either, students might look for long- and short-term examples, how causes or effects connect, their relative importance, and the roles played by different causes.	

Disciplinary concept	Description	Link
Change and continuity	Explores how things change or remain the same over time. This could include speed and scale of changes, changes against a set of criteria (progression, regression and stagnation) or discussions of particular moments of change, sometimes called 'turning points'.	
Similarity and difference	Examines variation within a time period. This might be considered in terms of events or thematic patterns, but often focuses on people of different social groups, considering class, gender, ethnicity, etc.	
Historical significance	Explores how and why events, individuals, processes and developments matter to, have meaning for or are ascribed meaning by people, both now and at different times in the past. In recent years, teachers have begun to include 'silence' as part of this concept, highlighting areas of the past that have hitherto not been deemed important, and the reasons for and effects of this, as well as reasons why these silences may now be challenged.	
Using sources of evidence	Develops students' understanding of primary source material and how it is used by historians. Considers how the evidence we take from sources is contextualised, analysed, interpreted and deployed in the historical process.	
Interpretations of the past	Focuses students' attention on constructed versions or representations of the past, ranging from museum displays to artistic reconstructions to academic scholarship. Analyses the interpretations conveyed, and the means of and reasons for their creation.	

▲ Figure A3.5: Disciplinary concepts in history

Developing students' disciplinary understanding is integral to the study of history. This is important not only because historians do it, or because it helps students write stronger exam answers in later years, but because it is key to the 'manifestation of history' in the classroom discussed in chapter A1. Wrestling with these disciplinary elements, arriving at judgements and testing these in an environment of challenging debate is where much of the joy of history is found, as we will see in chapter C3.

> Ofsted's 2021 research review for history discusses disciplinary knowledge in history in more detail, and the most relevant section can be found here:
>
>

Teachers of history therefore need to make time for the disciplinary thinking to be teased out of a story, discussed, argued and written about. Disciplinary thinking, done well, provokes curiosity and energises young minds to develop a meaningful understanding of the past. Without it, we are training chroniclers, not historians.

See chapters C1 and C2.

Use of enquiry questions to integrate disciplinary and substantive knowledge

Enquiry questions are used to govern learning across a sequence of lessons. Effective enquiry questions are genuine historical questions that integrate disciplinary and substantive knowledge throughout the lesson sequence.

> In the Historical Association's 'What's the Wisdom on… Enquiry Questions?', Rachel Foster's enquiry question, 'What's the story of the women's suffrage campaign?', uses a focus on interpretations to guide students through the topic of the women's suffrage campaign (Historical Association, 2020). In this enquiry, students consider how and why differing interpretations of the past arise, and examine developments in historiography and historians' methodologies (Historical Association, 2020).

Crafting enquiry questions requires detailed knowledge of the period and of relevant historical scholarship. This knowledge not only guides the selection of relevant content and the appropriate simplification of that content for a particular year group or class, but also informs the selection of an appropriate disciplinary lens through which students will study the past. A history teacher's knowledge supplies the fingertip knowledge needed to furnish students' historical understanding, and enables them to define the core knowledge students should take from the enquiry.

For further support and guidance on crafting and using enquiry questions, see:

In his pioneering article about curriculum planning at Key Stage 3, Michael Riley (2000) urged teachers to consider whether their enquiry questions worked collectively to:

- address the range of skill, knowledge and understanding required by the history curriculum
- blend outline and depth within and across enquiries to create more profound understanding
- reinforce each other in order to promote students' knowledge-building as they progress through Key Stage 3
- create patterns of reinforcement in historical thinking so that questions of the same type will resonate with students, teasing out old learning.

> For further examples of history teachers using enquiry questions in this way, see: Historical Association (2020); Riley (2000); Byrom and Riley (2003); Burnham and Brown (2004; 2014); Brown, Fordham and Stanford (2012); Worth (2018); Richards (2019).

To demonstrate how an enquiry can integrate disciplinary and substantive knowledge, and manage the interplay between the two, we will return to the substantive concept of 'revolution' and examine a three-lesson enquiry on the Russian Revolution. This unit will appear as part of the curriculum overview in chapter B3. It sits near the start of the Year 9 course.

Enquiry question: How did Russia become the world's first communist state?					
Structural element	Builds on from Year 7/8/9	Taught in the Year 9 unit itself			Builds towards (Year 9, GCSE and A-level)
		Lesson 1: causes	Lesson 2: events	Lesson 3: consequences	
Substantive knowledge	Year 8: examples of political revolutions and common causes of them (poverty, representation, war)	situation in Russia 1900–1917	events of February 1917 events of October 1917	1920s and 1930s in Russia – Civil War, policies of Lenin and Stalin signposts to Second World War, Cold War, 20th-century Russia	Year 9: - 1920s and 1930s - causes of Second World War - Cold War - decolonisation GCSE: rise of Nazis
Substantive concepts	Year 7: medieval social hierarchy and systems of landholding Year 8: nature of revolutions – English Civil War, America, France, Haiti	class poverty hierarchy aristocracy monarchy democracy	popular revolution vs coup d'état	civil war totalitarian/police state dictatorship	GCSE and A-level: spread of communism and perception of it as a danger to west
Disciplinary concepts	Year 7/8: understanding of cause and consequence Year 9: reinforce multi-causal explanations after causes of First World War enquiry	long- and short-term causes role of individuals		long- and short-term consequences national and international consequences	GCSE and A-level: writing about cause and consequence

▲ Figure A3.6: Example of integration of substantive and disciplinary knowledge in a three-lesson enquiry

This short enquiry does far more than tell the story of the Russian revolution. It provides an opportunity to reinforce some substantive concepts, such as revolution, as well as a chance to explore new ones, especially communism. This unit secures students' conceptual understanding of consequence, by exploring how the Russian revolution grew from the First World War and Russian societal context. The idea of long- and short-term consequences is revisited at later stages of the Year 9 curriculum, for example in units about the Second World War and the Cold War (see chapter B3).

There are no quick wins when it comes to resolving the relationship between the substantive and disciplinary in a curriculum. Wrestling with the challenges illustrated in figure A3.6 is part of the joy of curriculum design in history, and excellent history curricula are, in part, a product of this thought process. See chapter C3 for examples of some departments' approaches to negotiating this interplay.

Planning for interplay between categories of historical knowledge across a curriculum

Cumulatively, the curriculum should plan for progression in students' substantive and disciplinary knowledge across a key stage via the sequence of enquiry questions they answer. As Riley (2000) argued, we must consider how our enquiry questions look collectively.

Establishing a curriculum-wide relationship between the substantive and disciplinary is complex. There is no blueprint for the selection of content, neither is there a blueprint for how students' disciplinary knowledge should progress. Teachers must therefore give consideration to three things:

1. how 'one layer of substantive knowledge will accelerate another' (Counsell, 2017)
2. how and when students' disciplinary knowledge is developed
3. how substantive knowledge is used to support students' learning of disciplinary knowledge (Ofsted, 2021).

The Ofsted research review for history argues that the second consideration in the list can be particularly problematical because 'pupils must have secure and detailed prior knowledge of at least two different domains – the specific substantive context or topic and the relevant disciplinary knowledge – to understand and learn more complex disciplinary knowledge' (Ofsted, 2021).

A further issue is that of assessment. Ideally, assessment will allow students to demonstrate integration of substantive and disciplinary knowledge. This is a key reason for criticism of skill-based level descriptors (Ofsted, 2021). See Part D for further discussion of assessment in history.

CHAPTER A4
CONVERSATIONS IN THE HISTORY SUBJECT COMMUNITY

History teachers are lucky to have a vibrant and engaged subject community. This community fulfils a crucial function by discussing, debating and theorising how the discipline of history is mediated and taught in schools. As chapter A2 demonstrates, school history is constantly evolving. This is because history teachers are far from reaching a consensus on a number of questions and challenges relating to history teaching. This chapter outlines some of the conversations taking place in our subject community at the time of writing. Understanding developments in history teaching over time provides the context for the conversations and debates that occupy history educators; this is key to informed curriculum development and delivery.

Conversations about diversification and decolonisation of school history curricula

Voices in the history teaching community have long called for school history curricula to incorporate or be informed by global perspectives (Priggs, 2020). In recent years, these calls have grown in number. Michael Gove's proposed changes to the national curriculum in 2013, which focused narrowly on a political narrative of British history, were just one factor prompting history teachers to pay more attention to the diversity of their curriculum. As a result not only have many departments widened the scope of their Key Stage 3 curriculum, but exam boards have also widened the scope of their specifications. Since the introduction of new GCSE specifications in 2016, AQA, Edexcel and OCR have all created GCSE units on migration.

See chapter B1.

This change has been driven by several factors. Some history teachers have argued that the curriculum should embrace multiculturalism so that students are able to see themselves in the curriculum and understand our shared past (Traille, 2007). Similarly, the past is diverse and therefore teaching a diverse past is 'good' history (Priggs, 2020). Criticism of the narrowness of history curricula from historians such as David Olusoga and from the Royal Historical Society led to calls for better teaching of Black history and the empire (Olusoga, 2016; RHS, 2018). As the number of school history departments responding to this call has grown, so has the debate about how to bring marginalised voices into the classroom. Voices within and outside the history teaching community have called for curricula to be 'diversified' and 'decolonised'. These terms are not mutually exclusive, but it is worth exploring what each might look like in practice.

Diversification of the curriculum

Diversification of the curriculum tends to follow one of two approaches:

1. Topics taught are re-evaluated to add depth to existing narratives

Some teachers seek to re-conceptualise familiar topics by adding complexity. This allows dominant narratives and interpretations to be challenged, and more nuanced and representative histories can be created. A good example of this is the incorporation of Black British history into the mainstream history curriculum, which several teachers have advocated and exemplified in their own work (Lyndon-Cohen, 2006; Whitburn and Yemoh, 2012; Dennis, 2017; Cusworth, 2021).

In some cases, this stems from the use of new historical scholarship to underpin curriculum planning: new lenses or perspectives on seemingly well-known topics have motivated a desire to refresh teaching. Miranda Kaufmann's *Black Tudors*, for example, has inspired many to reframe or change the emphasis of their teaching of Tudor England (Kaufmann, 2017).

2. Diverse cultures and civilisations from across the world are taught in their own right

An alternative way to diversify a curriculum is to teach non-British cultures and civilisations discretely. This approach is discussed in the next section.

World history

With a renewed focus on curriculum design overall, the scope of the curriculum has received growing attention in recent years. Some departments have modified the scope of their curriculum, introducing new topics, while others have made more sweeping changes. But there is more than one way to broaden the scope of a history curriculum. One possible approach is to broaden the scope of study to include greater geographical breadth and a more diverse range of cultures and civilisations across the world. This is sometimes referred to as 'world history'.

Teachers including world history in the curriculum have often been motivated by the desire to encourage the study of civilisations in their own right. This has been particularly compelling in the recent past as departments have considered the status ascribed to other civilisations by their curriculum and have sought to 'decolonise' their approach to history. In light of this, a curriculum incorporating topics from 'world history' may appeal to teachers because it offers the opportunity to reframe the history of other civilisations and to avoid portraying these only through a colonial lens, or as adjuncts or precursors to empire.

A history of world history

This approach is not entirely new, however. A world history-inspired approach has been discernible in history classrooms since the 1970s. In 1991, England's national curriculum for history introduced a required unit on 'world history', listing options such as 'Islamic civilisations', 'Imperial China' and 'Mughal India' (DfE, 1990).

Extensive studies of world civilisations have not been widely adopted, but history teachers have continued to debate how to teach a range of world civilisations:

- Abdul Mohamud and Robin Whitburn have made a compelling case for history teachers to do justice to the teaching of Black history by moving away from introducing African history with a 'sense of victimhood or western dominance' (Mohamud and Whitburn, 2016).
- William Bailey-Watson and Richard Kennett's 'Meanwhile, elsewhere...' project has seen the compilation of resources created by teachers to enable students to take a 'sideways glance' at the history of another place, concurrent with their primary topic of study. For example, when students study the Norman Conquest, they can expand their horizons by looking at the Song Dynasty (Bailey-Watson and Kennett, 2019).
- David Hibbert and Zaiba Patel threaded Indian history throughout their Key Stage 3 curriculum with specific units presenting case studies (Hibbert and Patel, 2019).
- World history has more of a foothold in the US education system, where American and world history are often taught as separate subjects. Ross Dunn (2008) categorised approaches to teaching world history into two 'arenas', summarised in figure A4.1.

Arena A	Arena B
Advocates aim for students to learn about cultures and civilisations with a view to uncovering a unified history of mankind. One method of doing this is to emphasise connections across civilisations (Manning, 2003).	Advocates debate whether world history should be used to teach 'western heritage' or with a view to fostering multiculturalism and anti-racism.

▲ Figure A4.1: Categorising approaches to teaching world history (Dunn, 2008)

A series of textbooks edited by Christine Counsell takes the approach advocated by the scholars and teachers Dunn places in Arena A (Counsell et al., 2024b). The *Changing Histories* series seeks to reframe traditional Key Stage 3 curriculum routes by emphasising connections between culture and civilisations; 'hidden' voices are uncovered as part of this reframing.

Reconciling approaches to teaching a diverse past

When executed successfully, either approach identified by Dunn should avoid examples of diverse history being 'bolted on' to the existing curriculum. A 'bolt-on' approach can actually further marginalise other voices or perspectives (Hibbert and Patel, 2019; Priggs, 2020). Careful consideration should therefore be given to the emplotment of diverse and representative topics through the curriculum, considering how these are integrated with the rest of the curriculum.

Decolonisation of the curriculum

Some practitioners have called for history curricula to be decolonised (Lyndon-Cohen, 2021). Here, the emphasis is on critical analysis of a curriculum, identifying where or how colonial worldviews are dominant in narratives and interpretations, or where these underpin the design of the curriculum, and working actively to challenge and deconstruct these views. This process aims to make space for other ways of thinking and to uncover silences in the history that has been told and taught; it has been used by some teachers to prompt students to question what they are being taught.

Involving students in diversification and decolonisation of the history curriculum

Teachers and academics have called for the curriculum to hold personal significance for students (Cusworth, 2021; Traille, 2007). This has led some to consider the role of pupil voice in curriculum construction (Priggs, 2020). Moreover, some advocates of 'decolonising' the history curriculum aim to furnish students' curiosity and their ability to ask questions about what they have studied (Lyndon-Cohen, 2021).

Conversations about the use of academic historical scholarship

Historical scholarship is the work of historians. Scholarship is a product of research, created to communicate new historical knowledge and interpretations. History teachers using academic historical scholarship in the classroom has been a growing trend in recent years. Scholarship can be used to engage students with the discipline of history in a direct and rigorous way. Teachers using academic scholarship with their students have had a number of disciplinary rationales for doing so, including:

Historical scholarship allows students to interact with genuine and live historical claims

Reading historical scholarship involves students in the discourse of historians. Several factors, including time pressure, may encourage teachers to fall back on topics and lines of enquiry that are 'safe' because they are familiar, established and well-resourced. In some cases, these topics and resources may not reflect the current state of scholarship or live areas of debate on a topic; using recent historical scholarship avoids the rehearsal to students of out-of-date historical claims or evidence, and ensures that the curriculum reflects what is current in the discipline.

Historical scholarship models the discipline by showing students what historians do

Engaging with scholarship shows students what history is and what historians do. Teachers can use historical scholarship to build students' disciplinary knowledge. An extract from historical scholarship might be used to show students what a sophisticated causal argument looks like and how it is built. An extract might reveal how historians use different lenses through which to study and perceive the past, and how some use multiple lenses. Scholarship can exemplify what scale-changing looks like in practice, how historians make use of evidence, and the different types of evidence they use, or how a historian subtly and meaningfully blends alternative narratives with mainstream accounts.

Historical scholarship shows students that history is constructed and contested

Recognition that history is a construct is crucial to students' understanding of the subject. Historians revisit, affirm, disrupt and contest existing claims when constructing their own. Understanding this will help students to appreciate the status of knowledge in history and how and why differing historical claims arise. Choosing the right scholarship can demonstrate this process perfectly.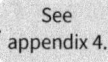

Historical scholarship helps to obviate misconceptions and challenge preconceptions

Grounding our teaching in scholarship ensures that we do not perpetuate unsubstantiated or outdated historical claims and can help to prevent students developing misconceptions about history and the past. Moreover, scholarship can be used to challenge the preconceptions of both students and teachers. This is especially important when new historical interpretations are formed in light of new evidence becoming available, or when historians reinterpret the past through a different lens or using a different historical method.

Historical scholarship can be a good vehicle for teaching emotive and controversial history

Teachers need to be sensitive to how emotive and controversial history will land in the classroom and be prepared to challenge perceptions and misconceptions. The *Teaching Emotional and Controversial History Report* (Wrenn et al., 2013) argues that scholarship can be used to ground debates in evidence and highlight differing views.

How to use scholarship

Scholarship can be used to underpin curriculum planning and development. For example:

- Having identified confidence and passion for reading as a way to build his students' historical knowledge, Tim Jenner transformed his team's Key Stage 3 curriculum by using scholarship to inform every enquiry (Jenner, 2019). The same approach was taken by Rachel Burney and her team at Stanground Academy in Peterborough (figure A4.2).
- Hibbert and Patel used the scholarship of historian Yasmin Khan to shape a Year 9 sequence of lessons on experiences of the Second World War (Hibbert and Patel, 2019). Not only did they see the benefit of using scholarship to guide curriculum planning, they also wanted to encourage their students to think more deeply about how historians work, including the ways in which they work with evidence.
- Alex Ford was concerned about students' ability to discern narrative in the content-heavy GCSE specifications (Ford, 2019). He used historical scholarship as a 'narrative core', which he hoped would allow students to see the bigger picture and provide them with a chronological framework.

SECONDARY HISTORY IN ACTION

Year 7	7.1 What's so special about Oswald's arm?	7.2 Tang Golden Age	7.3 Did the Normans change what it meant to be English?	7.4 How and why did ideas spread around the medieval world?
Scholarship links/background reading	*The King in the North* – Max Adams	*China's Golden Age: everyday life in the Tang Dynasty* – Charles Benn	*The Anglo-Saxons: a history of the beginnings of England* – Marc Morris *The Norman Conquest: the battle of Hastings and the fall of Anglo-Saxon England* – Marc Morris	*The Map of Knowledge: how classical ideas were lost and found: a history in seven cities* – Violet Möller
Year 8	8.1 Why did Luther's ideas spread so far and so fast?	8.2 How much can paintings reveal about life in the Mughal Empire?	8.3 How dramatically did the Civil War change England?	8.4 Why was slavery abolished in the British Empire?
Scholarship links/ background reading	*Reformation: Europe's house divided 1490–1700* – Diarmaid MacCulloch	*Courting India: England, Mughal India and the origins of empire* – Nandini Das *The Great Mughals: art, architecture and opulence* – Susan Stronge	*Civil War: the history of England* – Peter Ackroyd	*Sugar in the Blood: a family's story of slavery and empire* – Andrea Stuart *Black and British: a short essential history* – David Olusoga
Year 9	9.1 How has Hallie Rubenhold rewritten the story of the Whitechapel murders?	9.2 What was the significance of the Treaty of Versailles for international relations?	9.3 How far did the 1920 roar for all Americans?	9.5 Why did the Nazis come to power?
Scholarship links / background reading	*The Five: the untold lives of the women killed by Jack the Ripper* – Hallie Rubenhold	*The Long Shadow: the Great War and the twentieth century* – David Reynolds	*Anything Goes: a biography of the Roaring Twenties* – Lucy Moore	*The Weimar Years: rise and fall 1918–1933* – Frank McDonough

*students read extended extracts from these works of scholarship

▲ Figure A4.2: Key Stage 3 overview from Stanground Academy, Peterborough, showing background reading and historical scholarship used in the curriculum, with thanks to Rachel Burney

7.5 What can the story of Mansa Musa reveal about medieval West Africa?	7.6 What were the greatest consequences of the Black Death on medieval society?	7.7 How did women fight the Wars of the Roses?	7.8 Who were the Tudors?
The Empires of Medieval West Africa: Ghana, Mali and Songhay – David Conrad	**The Black Death: a personal history* – John Hatcher	*Blood Sisters: the women behind the Wars of the Roses* – Sarah Gristwood	*Black Tudors: the untold story* – Miranda Kaufmann *Disability and the Tudors: all the king's fools* – Philippa Vincent-Connolly
8.6 What was the most significant advancement in medicine?	8.7 How far was 1838 a year of freedom?	8.8 When did Britain become a democracy?	8.9 How far have migrants been welcome to Britain over time?
Unwell Women – Elinor Cleghorn *The Butchering Art: Joseph Lister's quest to transform the grisly world of Victorian medicine* – Lindsey Fitzharris	*Ruling the World: freedom, civilisation and liberalism in the nineteenth-century British Empire* – Alan Lester, Kate Boehme and Peter Mitchell	*British General Election Campaigns 1830–2019: the 50 general election campaigns that shaped our modern politics* – Iain Dale	**Black and British: a short essential history* – David Olusoga *Rebuilding Post-War Britain: Latvian, Lithuanian and Estonia refugees in Britain* – Emily Gilbert
9.6 What kind of change was experienced by ordinary people in Stalin's Russia?	9.7 How far were all Germans 'Hitler's Willing executioners?'	9.8 What can sources reveal about how Britain was rebuilt after the Second World War?	9.9 How did different countries experience the Cold War?
*The Whisperers: private life in Stalin's Russia – Orlando Figes	**Hitler's Willing Executioners: Ordinary Germans and the Holocaust* – Daniel Goldhagen **ordinary men* – Christopher Browning	*Rebuilding Post War Britain: Latvian, Lithuanian and Estonian refugees in Britain, 1946–51* – Emily Gilbert	*The Cold War: a very short introduction* – Robert J. McMahon

These teachers, despite taking different approaches, all demonstrate how scholarship can be used as an integral feature of curriculum design, rather than as an ad hoc feature of individual lessons. Research suggests that fewer and more frequent encounters with the same historian or piece of scholarship builds students' capacity to read and access academic texts (Jenner, 2019).

Another common feature of these approaches is that teachers used scholarship to address a curricular deficit. Their use of scholarship was driven not only by a commitment to 'good history', but in response to students' needs.

Barriers to students' accessing academic historical scholarship

It is crucial to acknowledge and consider barriers that may hinder students' ability to access scholarship. Jenner identified four factors that influence students' reading (figure A4.3), arguing that consideration of these factors can make academic historical scholarship accessible to all (Jenner, 2019).

Vocabulary	Background knowledge
Most academic texts are likely to include a significant amount of unfamiliar Tier 3 vocabulary (subject-specific words). Challenging texts are also rich in Tier 2 vocabulary (words which are uncommon in everyday, spoken language but often appear in academic texts), and pupils' security in this vocabulary greatly affects their ability to read texts. Pupils need to be familiar with most of this vocabulary if they are to get the gist of the text.	Academic texts often assume a high level of 'background' knowledge. To understand what they are reading, pupils therefore need to already have a strong sense of period and rich contextual knowledge.
Form	**Motivation**
Pupils need a secure understanding of the form/structures/conventions of a type of text.	Pupils are more likely to persist with a challenging text if they have confidence in their own ability to read and a desire to read.

▲ Figure A4.3: Factors that influence pupils' experience of reading (taken from Jenner, 2019), with thanks to the Historical Association

Conversations about interpretations

Through their study of history students will not only learn about the past, they will learn how people subsequent to the periods they study have represented the past, through the production of historical interpretations; students will also learn why historians have chosen to represent the past in certain ways. This is the study of interpretations.

> For further discussion of disciplinary concepts see A3.

Studying interpretations is crucial to a rich history curriculum: it allows students to engage with, and understand, the very essence of history. Yet it is a contested and challenging aspect of history teaching. Analysis of the strengths and weaknesses of history education in England has repeatedly highlighted inconsistencies and weaknesses in approaches to teaching interpretations over two decades (Ofsted, 2007; 2011; 2023).

Debates about interpretations

Challenges history teachers face in teaching about interpretations include defining the nature of historical interpretations and the scope of their study, and deciding how students at secondary level should encounter and study them.

The nature of historical interpretations

There is some debate about what constitutes an historical interpretation. Some teachers focus on interpretations created by academic historians: the historical scholarship discussed in the previous section. The broader range of ways in which the past has been presented are also, however, interpretations. Many have advocated that students be introduced to this broader range of interpretations, such as 'popular accounts, folk histories, museums and films' (Ofsted, 2021). Figure A4.4, presented at the 2004 HMI conference on interpretations, includes further examples.

> For historical scholarship, see also 'Conversations in the history subject community: use of academic historical scholarship'.

A selection of interpretation types commonly examined by history teachers between 1991 and 2004	
Academic • Books, journals, papers by professional historians • Scholarly lectures • Excavation reports	Fictional/semi-fictional • Novels, paintings, plays • Films • TV drama/comedy
Educational • Textbooks • Museums and sites • Reconstructions • TV documentaries/news • CDs, websites, internet discussions, podcasts, blogs	Popular and/or political • Folk wisdom/personal reflection • Theme parks/souvenirs • Paintings of earlier periods • Monuments/ceremonies/protests • Advertising • Websites, magazines • Political speeches or arguments that invoke the past in some way

▲ Figure A4.4: History teachers' update of McAleavy's types (Historical Association, 2019), with thanks to the Historical Association

Interpretations: the disciplinary concept

Since the early 1990s, the Key Stage 3 national curriculum has included a focus on interpretations as a disciplinary concept. The current national curriculum states that students should 'understand the methods of historical enquiry, including how evidence is used rigorously to make historical claims, and discern how and why contrasting arguments and interpretations of the past have been constructed' (DfE, 2013).

Yet these disciplinary aims are sometimes misunderstood. Ofsted's 2023 research reported that asking students to form their own interpretations about the past was sometimes confused with a study of the craft of historians and evaluation of historical interpretations (Ofsted, 2023).

Interpretations at GCSE

There is a requirement for students to engage with historical interpretations at GCSE. The assessment objectives (AO4) require students to 'Analyse, evaluate and make substantiated judgements about interpretations (including how and why interpretations may differ) in the context of historical events studied.' (Edexcel, 2016; AQA, 2021; OCR, 2023).[1]

Despite clarity in exam specifications about what constitutes historical interpretations, some of the ways in which students' knowledge and understanding of interpretations are assessed in examinations have been criticised for a lack of rigour relative to the treatment of interpretations at Key Stage 3.

Furthermore, one of the key laments of Ofsted's 2023 research related to the influence of GCSE specifications on history teaching at Key Stage 3: 'the teaching of disciplinary knowledge in Key Stage 3 was overly influenced by leaders' interpretations of GCSE examination requirements' (Ofsted, 2023). Students' interaction with interpretations offers an opportunity to learn about and engage in the disciplinary processes involved in the construction of interpretations. They need not be limited to 'making simplistic judgements on individual sources rather than learning how historians construct accounts' (Ofsted, 2023).

Evidence and interpretations

See chapter A3. For further detail see 'What's the Wisdom on… Evidence and Sources' (Historical Association, 2019).

The important distinction between 'evidence' and 'interpretations', and between students' work with primary sources and with subsequent accounts, was highlighted in the 1991 national curriculum (DES, 1991). Students need to ask and answer different questions about primary source material and about subsequent interpretations, and these different types of material are also used in the classroom to different ends. For example, students will learn to use sources as evidence to support or challenge an historical claim, and how historians cite evidence in support of their own interpretation or to challenge those of others.

Tony McAleavy contributed to the discourse about interpretations in the classroom by arguing that the study of interpretations must be distinguished from forming one's own view or interpretation of the past (McAleavy, 1993). For students to be able to produce a genuinely historical analysis of interpretations (i.e. to think critically about how different interpretations come about) teachers need to recognise that the construction of interpretations combines 'fact and fiction, imagination and points of view', that interpretations are dependent on evidence, and

---

[1] It is worth noting that despite it being a key component of the Key Stage 3 history curriculum, it was not until the revised specifications of 2015 onwards that exam boards used this definition of historical interpretations.

that the provenance of an interpretation can help to explain differences between interpretations (McAleavy, 1993).

Tackling interpretations in the classroom

For examples of teachers working with students on interpretations, see:

There are numerous examples of teachers engaging students in the study of interpretations. Michael Fordham asked his Year 9 students 'Why did Dr Seuss write the Butter Battle Book in 1984?' to prompt them to learn that periods of the past 'can be interpreted in different ways for a specific purpose' (Fordham, 2014). Samuel Head used the visual metaphor of an iceberg to support his A-level students 'to develop "intuitive habits" for approaching interpretations' (Head, 2020). Head's diagram began with surface-level questions, such as 'What claims does the historian make?', becoming steadily more complex and building students' understanding of the context of the interpretation and methodology of the historian, before arriving at 'What questions are being asked by the historian?' (Head, 2020). Ofsted's findings from existing research suggest that to engage with interpretations effectively, 'pupils require secure substantive knowledge of two contexts – the events or period described in the interpretation, and the context in which the interpretation was constructed' (Ofsted, 2021). Jane Card described 'one historical period's visualisation of another' as 'double vision'. She argued that students need to 'see double' due to their analysis of two periods – the period of the past represented in the interpretation and the period within which the interpretation was produced (Card, 2004).

At GCSE and A-level, students need to understand the 'how and why' of interpretations of the past. The Historical Association argues this is crucial to understanding interpretations for two reasons: first, because 'interpretations are always created for a reason and in a particular context', and second, because '...an interpretation is always a social process... It is part of a dialogue over time' (Historical Association, 2019). These two characteristics help to distinguish interpretations from sources and indicate the types of questions students need to ask when evaluating interpretations.

Figure A4.5 offers a tool to support teachers when planning how to teach interpretations in the curriculum. Notably, students should not ask all the suggested questions simultaneously; rather, the range of questions should inform students' interaction with interpretations across a key stage, including the wording of enquiry questions (Historical Association, 2019).

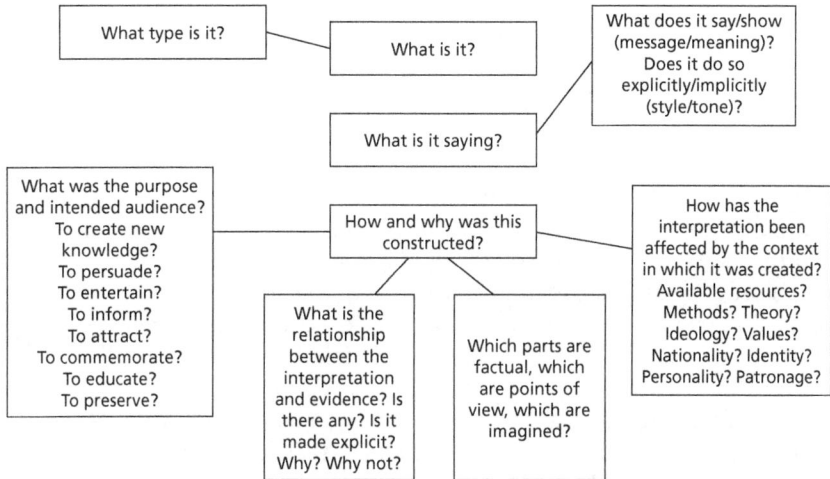

▲ **Figure A4.5:** A guide to shaping questions in the study of interpretations (Historical Association, 2019) with thanks to the Historical Association

Finally, history teachers need to safeguard against students evaluating historical interpretations as they would primary sources. Fordham found that his students slipped into 'applying a "reliability" or "accuracy" framework to historical argument' when studying historical interpretations (Fordham, 2007). Making use of questions presented in figure A4.5 will support students critically to engage with historical interpretations, and avoid students ascribing to them the same status as primary sources, or interrogating them in the same way.

> For further practical guidance on how to teach students about historical interpretations see the Historical Association's 'What's the Wisdom on… Interpretations of the Past' (Historical Association, 2019).

CHAPTER A5
PROGRESSION IN HISTORY

What does it mean to get better at history? The answer ultimately rests on what we think history is and what we think it is for. To say that history teachers want students to make progress in history implies that there is a gold standard of history that we aspire for students to attain. Peter Lee (2017) urged that 'while classroom activities do matter, they can be futile unless they fit into a clear conception of what history education ought to be'. As we saw in chapter A4, however, many aspects of school history teaching are the subject of ongoing debate, discussion and development. There is no unified consensus about the purpose or endpoints of school history, or how it should be achieved.

> For more on the purpose of school history and the ongoing conversations about this, see chapters A1 and A4.

Fewer than half of students in England go on to study history at GCSE, so thinking about the purpose of school history must involve thinking about the endpoints for these students, at the end of Year 9, or even the end of Year 8, as well as planning for progression for students who continue to study history at GCSE and post-16. The national curriculum for history in England outlines both substantive and disciplinary endpoints for students' knowledge and understanding (Department for Education, 2014). Where history departments have additional aims for their curriculum, these will also inform the endpoints for their students. Jonathan Grande (2023) engaged his department in debating and defining the aims of their history curriculum in order to define the endpoints or takeaways towards which students should progress.

> See chapter A1 and appendix 3.

Progression in substantive knowledge

To plan for progression in students' substantive knowledge, it is helpful to think about the residue of knowledge that students will retain by the end of a term, a year or a key stage. Ian Dawson introduced the idea of takeaways when he argued that 'the key to coherence and progression is planning backwards, having first identified what we hope and intend students will take away from their Key Stage 3 history' (Dawson, 2008). In *Exploring and Teaching Medieval History* (2008), Dawson asked historians what they would like students to know and understand about the medieval period. The term 'takeaways', rather than outcomes or endpoints, conveys the idea that students have an entitlement to take something away from their history education into the rest of their lives.

The examples Dawson compiled are ambitious. They frame big understandings: the residue of knowledge that students will retain, not the fingertip knowledge, the small stories, that get them there in the first place. As such, these takeaways do not tell teachers *how* to help students make progress, but defining what we want students to make progress *towards* is a vital first step. Jonathan Grande used Dawson's principles to define the takeaways he wanted his students to have at key endpoints over the course of his curriculum (Grande, 2023).

The value of substantive knowledge in securing progression for students in history has been demonstrated in research by Kate Hammond. Hammond (2014) found that her students' success at GCSE was underpinned by substantive knowledge that went well beyond knowledge of the topic on the GCSE specification. She wrote about how this knowledge manifested itself indirectly in the work of her most successful students.

We can think about how students make progress in their substantive knowledge and their understanding of substantive concepts by thinking about how repeated encounters with concepts – made concrete, meaningful and memorable through stories – build students' schemata for these concepts. Students begin to form an understanding of parliament, for example, on first encountering the word, probably at primary school. Further encounters with this word through stories, when studying medieval England and the early modern period, deepen their understanding and begin to facilitate the development of a nuanced schema that accounts for the shifting meaning of the word over time, from the earliest parliaments of the 13th century to the present day. Sally Burnham and Geraint Brown (2004) reflected on how richer knowledge of stories, cultures and periods deepens and develops students' understanding of abstract concepts such as empire.

Secure knowledge of substantive concepts seems to be fundamental to progression in history. Alexander Bridges (2018) and Dominic Palek (2015) both researched students' understanding of substantive concepts such as parliament or ideology, and both concluded that students'

43

progression in forming and supporting historical claims about causation or change relies on secure knowledge of substantive concepts. Planning for the development of students' substantive knowledge is the work of curriculum planning. Jacob Olivey (2021) illustrated how he planned for a coherent sequence of progression in students' substantive knowledge in his curriculum, drawing on the research of Burnham, Brown and others. In other words, in Fordham's (2020) phrase, 'the curriculum is the progression model'.

See chapter A3, *WalkThrus* 1 Coherent mapping and Ofsted's research review for history:

Progression in disciplinary understanding

After discussing the importance of students building a substantive 'picture of the past', Lee (2017) tacks on the observation that history is conceptually counter-intuitive. Sam Wineburg, similarly, has described historical thinking as an 'unnatural act' (Wineburg, 2001). Cognitive bias, specifically the 'curse of expertise', may lead history teachers to overlook the extent to which students may misconceive the nature of history and its relationship to the past. Those misconceptions include the belief that direct experience is the best, or even the only, way to know something, and that there can be only one history because there was only one past. We therefore need to plan for the curriculum to develop students' knowledge and understanding of history as a discipline – including their ability to distinguish history from the past – as well as their substantive knowledge; something that Lee warns does not just come with repeated practice (Lee, 2017).

Research modelling progression

Hammond's 2014 research focused on the development of her students' substantive knowledge and its effect on the quality of their historical thinking and writing. The same principle can be applied to progression in disciplinary understanding, however. Repeated practice of examination questions focusing on causation or change/continuity does not secure progression. Rather, when students answer these questions well in examinations, showing conceptual understanding of causation or change, this is a manifestation of their accumulation of a depth of conceptual understanding of these disciplinary concepts.

For disciplinary concepts, see A3.

History teachers have turned to models of the discipline of history – to the work of historians – to identify how historians write about different disciplinary concepts, and how these approaches can provide a guide for curricular planning for progression. For example, Matthew Stanford (2019) and James Carroll (2018a; 2022) have each explored the causal models historians use, while Paula Worth (2023) analysed how historians write about historical significance. The work of these and many other history educators has established a wealth of professional knowledge in relation to disciplinary concepts in the history classroom, supporting teachers to define ambitious takeaways for their students. Tom Morton and Peter Seixas (2013) also researched how students' understanding of the discipline progresses, identifying thresholds of thinking that students cross as their conceptual understanding develops. The difficulty in planning for progression, however, lies in sequencing students' encounters with each concept to achieve the desired outcomes.

Linear and non-linear progression models

Since the introduction of the first attainment targets for history in the 1991 national curriculum, successive attempts have been made to sequence the knowledge and understanding students should develop about each disciplinary concept into a linear hierarchy. These hierarchies of 'skill' have subsequently been converted into mark schemes and used to assess students' progress. These attempts have failed because the hierarchies created are flawed and because listing these endpoints of disciplinary knowledge and understanding, hierarchically or otherwise, does not describe the journey students need to take to achieve this understanding. Burnham and Brown (2004) analysed how an attempt to think about progression in causal reasoning as a series of incremental steps does not adequately model the way in which students develop their understanding of causation. Different aspects of disciplinary thinking are not inherently more or less challenging than one another. Moreover, different causal models, for example, are applicable to different causal questions. The challenge lies not only in the disciplinary concept but also in the substantive content and how these two are interwoven in the construction of historical narrative and argument. Students may be able to rank the causes of the Peasants' Revolt of 1381, but this does not mean they can do the same for the causes of the First World War.

> For more on this see:
>
> - chapters A3 and A4
> - Michael Fordham's blog, 'What did I mean by "the curriculum is the progression model"?'
> - Historical Association (2021) 'What's the Wisdom on… History Assessment?', *Teaching History 185*.

Students are on a linear journey through our curriculum, so a linear model of progression is appealing. Yet Morton and Seixas (2013) advocate thinking about progression in a non-linear way. Students' disciplinary knowledge and understanding may not progress in a predetermined sequence but will become more sophisticated over time. So how do we work with this non-linear model of progression in our curriculum and plan for progression in a more three-dimensional, multi-stranded, iterative way?

Stanford (2019) analysed the complexity of causal models involved in answering several different causal questions, and used this to inform his curriculum planning. He planned for students to encounter a series of causal questions over the course of the curriculum, each involving an increasingly complex causal model. Carroll (2018a; 2022), meanwhile, explored the use of metaphors and counterfactuals, and designed his curriculum to introduce students to these models of thinking about causation. Thus, curriculum planning can create opportunities for students to encounter and engage with different, and increasingly complex, causal models over time.

A similar approach can be used to plan for progression in other disciplinary concepts. Repeated encounters with questions about change/continuity, similarity/difference, evidence, historical significance or interpretations can be planned to ensure that over the course of the curriculum, students consider different facets of these disciplinary concepts and do so in an increasingly sophisticated way. In this way, the curriculum itself becomes a model for students' progression in history.

Part B

CHAPTER B1
HISTORY CURRICULUM PLANNING IN ACTION

Selecting content for a history curriculum is not a simple task. A department might start by considering the substantive knowledge they would like students to have acquired by the end of their compulsory study of history. Consideration would also need to be given to what would be studied at GCSE and post-16, seeing Key Stage 3 as the opportunity to develop foundational knowledge. With a strong foundation from Key Stage 3, students can specialise in later studies. A department might therefore start by considering their examination courses and work backwards.

See chapters A1 and A5 for an introduction to the debates about the purposes of history curricula.

While either, or both, of these starting points might feature in departments' conversations about curriculum content, to consider substantive knowledge alone would be far too simplistic, for studying history is much more than learning about the 'stuff' of the past. Selecting content cannot be separated from other curricular considerations; rather, it should be informed by them.

Key elements of history curriculum design

Key considerations in history curriculum design are scope, coherence, rigour and sequencing (figure B1.1). These inform the selection of content, both substantive and disciplinary, during the process of curriculum design.

Scope	Coherence
This refers to how far a curriculum reaches in several ways. For example, how far across time, how far across the world, and whether it embraces social, ethnic and religious diversity.	A curriculum is more than the sum of its parts. Topics in a curriculum should be 'held together'. A coherent narrative should be established through a curriculum, and connections between parts of the curriculum should be visible, obvious and sensible.

Rigour	Sequencing
A curriculum should offer an appropriate level of challenge. This may be manifest in, for example, fidelity to scholarship, the richness of detail, or the interplay of substantive and disciplinary knowledge. (For further discussion of this interplay, see chapter A3.)	Curriculum sequencing can be planned with careful intention to construct students' schemata of knowledge. The sequence of topics in a curriculum should create a coherent narrative. History lends itself to a chronologically-ordered narrative, but consideration should also be given to how students' interaction with substantive concepts is sequenced and how each new topic or enquiry builds on foundations previously laid.

▲ Figure B1.1 Key considerations in history curriculum design

For further exploration of each of these elements see Ofsted's research review series for history:

Appendix 2 shares a series of questions designed by Geraint Brown to support curriculum analysis and evaluation.

While these principles offer a framework for curriculum design, they do not prescribe particular content. All curricular planning should be underpinned by a department's vision for the aims and purposes of history in their students' education. Each member of the team should have a common understanding of the purpose of the curriculum – how the curriculum will change students by the end of each key stage (Richards, 2019). This will influence decisions about the content selected.

Even with consideration of the principles in figure B1.1, and a robust vision communicated and understood, decisions about content are still fraught with difficulty. Christine Counsell argues that decisions about what knowledge to teach are 'an exercise of power and therefore a weighty ethical responsibility' (Counsell, 2018). Selecting content for a curriculum is contentious. Answers to the question of what school history is *for* vary across and within schools and lead to debates about curriculum content.

Additional contextual factors influence decisions about the substance of a curriculum. These include teacher expertise in a department, new developments in historical scholarship, and factors specific to individual schools, such as the school's context and community, and curriculum time available. In short, when selecting content for a history curriculum, there is much for history departments to consider.

> For an example of the depth of thinking one multi-academy trust has put into its 'curriculum foundations' see appendix 3 for Jonathan Grande's 'Secondary History Design Architecture' document, which is used by Ark secondary schools. The extract focuses on the process of selecting content.

It is crucial that students know that a history curriculum is a product of selection, not the domain as a whole. Understanding the history curriculum as an interpretation is crucial for students' understanding of the nature of history as a discipline. Students should be able to discern, and should expect, that the narratives they encounter in the classroom are only *one* way of representing the past.

The scope, coherence, rigour and sequencing of a curriculum are closely interrelated. Curricular decisions will always involve compromise, and careful, thoughtful layering of knowledge. Departments should continually reflect upon and review their curriculum, treating curriculum design as an evolving, iterative process.

A useful consideration when planning for the progression of knowledge across a curriculum is how 'one layer of substantive knowledge will accelerate another' (Counsell, 2017). History teachers can use perennially limited curriculum time economically by planning for careful layering of knowledge that allows students to engage with substantive complexity and deep historical thinking more quickly and with greater richness. Olivey (2021) advocates for 'substantive coherence', planning for knowledge to

> 'work cumulatively and collectively across a curriculum to change how pupils "see" past worlds – and therefore change what they can "think" about them. This involves considering what new substantive knowledge builds upon and builds towards.'

This can work in a range of ways, including repeated encounters with geographical locations, tracing the lives of a member of a single family, or returning to a piece of technology or art. We can also plan for substantive and disciplinary knowledge to accelerate each other.

Scope, coherence and sequencing: geographic centres of gravity

Planning a curriculum so that students return to the same, familiar places over time has long been a popular approach. Jacob Olivey realised, however, that he could diversify his curriculum geographically and enhance its coherence by 'tracing how the same places developed and changed over vast expanses of time' (Olivey, 2021). As figure B1.2 shows, he chose Constantinople as a focus, and planned for his Year 7 curriculum to return there over the course of four separate enquiries. Crucial to the effectiveness of such an approach, Olivey has carefully considered the rationale for this choice so that it acts as a force for coherence in several ways. The choice of Constantinople facilitates ongoing encounters with the legacy of Rome as a way of understanding its lasting importance, and also demonstrates to students that the ancient and medieval worlds were deeply intertwined. A later enquiry on the Renaissance aims to knit together threads which emerged from the first three enquiries, on Pompeii, Constantinople as the new Rome and Constantinople under siege.

Enquiry	How students encounter Constantinople
2	Constantinople in the 6th century as a 'mighty trading port and intellectual powerhouse'
3	Constantinople under siege by the armies of the Umayyad Caliphate
5	Constantinople asking for help from Pope Urban II and later being sacked by the armies of the Fourth Crusade
7	The fall of Constantinople to the Ottomans

▲ Figure B1.2: An example of how, across a series of enquiries, students revisit a single location: Constantinople

Olivey's approach to scope and coherence illustrates just one approach, using one particular location as a coherent focus for a number of units of the curriculum for one year group. This example and its accompanying rationale demonstrate that curricular decisions of this kind require careful thought, attending to the implications of spending a significant amount of curriculum time on one particular place in the past. Taking this approach to its extreme could result in an unacceptable narrowing of the scope of the curriculum, to the detriment of students' historical understanding. Curriculum planning is, of necessity, a process of selection. Decisions about scope will inevitably require compromises and lead to absences and silences. These may be mitigated, and acknowledged, but not avoided entirely.

Rigour, sequencing and coherence: understanding how historians engage with evidence

See chapter A3 for an introduction to disciplinary concepts. See chapter A5 for the relationship between substantive and disciplinary knowledge in relation to progression.

For the most effective and efficient use of curriculum time allocated to history, it is crucial that teachers plan for disciplinary knowledge and substantive knowledge in relation to each other. Teachers can plan to build students' understanding of the relationship between the evidence and interpretations in the discipline of history by using concrete examples of the methods and work of particular historians (Hibbert and Patel, 2019). Introductory units isolating disciplinary concepts, asking 'What is history?' or similar questions, risk divorcing the work of historians from its substantive context. Beginning with a concrete example such as the work of Mary Beard on Pompeii can 'confront pupils with what it means to study the past which will provide them with a much richer understanding of the subject' (Hibbert and Priggs, 2021). The coherence and rigour of the curriculum can therefore be increased through repeated encounters with the aims, methods and evidence bases of historians in a range of substantive contexts (figure B1.3).

Stressing the importance of interplay between substantive and disciplinary knowledge was a key feature of Ofsted's research review for history. See chapter A2 for its place in the development of history teaching over time.

Enquiry 1	How does Mary Beard use archaeological evidence to come to conclusions about the lives of people in Pompeii?
Enquiry 2	How does the historian Toby Green use oral histories to reach conclusions about West Africa?
Enquiry 3	How does the historian Yasmin Khan use evidence to reach conclusions about experiences of the Second World War?

▲ Figure B1.3: An example of a series of enquiries each exploring how an historian uses evidence

Framing successive enquiries in this way ensures that students encounter different kinds of sources being used as evidence by historians in different ways. In the examples outlined in figure B1.3, students encounter oral history used by Toby Green in his research on West Africa, and later discuss its use by Yasmin Khan. In this second encounter, they also consider the limitations of recorded oral testimony for finding out about the lives of people in India during the Second World War. The layering of disciplinary knowledge in this way renders it more secure and flexible, making it possible to pose broader curricular questions, such as:

- How are the evidence bases for 16th-century England and 20th-century India similar and different?
- How are Yasmin Khan and Mary Beard different in their approaches?
- What difficulties might historians encounter when trying to answer questions about religious beliefs in Reformation Europe?

A coherent curriculum sequence can create opportunities to deepen students' engagement with and knowledge of the discipline. Once again, this relies on careful planning for the layering of disciplinary knowledge, as for the substantive.

Building a rich sense of period

When students lack a adequate knowledge of different places, people and periods in the past, this hinders their ability to make sense of and interpret the past, and makes misconceptions and anachronisms more likely. Curriculum planning can address this challenge. Mike Hill has theorised the importance of world building to build rich cognitive pictures of the past in the minds of students (Hill, 2020). This is a complex curricular aim, however, requiring attention throughout the curriculum.

World-building refers to the process by which teachers attempt to curate and construct an imagined past for students.

A strong sense of period has both proximal and relational dimensions. The proximal dimension involves students building cognitive pictures of a particular period or place. This might be planned into the curriculum through repeated encounters over the course of an enquiry with, for example, tenth century Baghdad. Through these repeated encounters which students build a picture of its architecture, geography and culture.

A relational sense of period involves building contrasting cognitive pictures so that students are able to draw comparisons, tracing change and continuity across periods and/or places, or identify similarities and differences between different places in the same time period. For example, an enquiry might be designed to build a picture of tenth-century London, in order to support students' ability to compare and contrast London and Baghdad in the same period. This relational dimension deepens students' sense of place and period by making connections between places and periods, providing more secure foundations for future study.

Exemplification using modes of transport

A relational or comparative sense of period might be developed by tracing an idea or theme through time (Ofsted, 2021). To give one example, across a number of units in a curriculum students might encounter the following stories featuring modes of transport within particular curricular contexts:

- Robert Beale carrying the death warrant of Mary Queen of Scots to Fotheringhay Castle by horse, in an enquiry about religious change in England 1500–1603
- Francis Drake's circumnavigation voyage of 1577–80, in an enquiry focused on sixteenth-century encounters
- the first journeys by rail and canal during the Industrial Revolution, in an enquiry on the extent of change for people in England 1700–1900
- the first supersonic flight by the Bell X-1 in 1947, in an enquiry on the origins of the Cold War.

Each of these stories serves both a proximal and a relational purpose. Each detail contributes to the layering of knowledge in each individual enquiry. When connections between periods are carefully drawn out by teachers in the classroom, these seemingly incidental details contribute to forming a broader comparative understanding of changes in modes of transportation over time, as well as of the political, social and economic impacts of the changes. In a carefully planned curriculum, the proximal and relational aspects of world building will interact and accumulate, building knowledge in an efficient and economical way in the curriculum time available.

Hill has also recently demonstrated how world-building can contribute to enriching students' disciplinary knowledge. He planned an enquiry using the story of photographer Sergey Prokudin-Gorsky, who was employed to take photographs of the Russian Empire in the early twentieth century in all its diversity. Hill uses the fascinating, vivid photographs taken by

Prokudin-Gorsky as a tool to build a mental model, while also building students' disciplinary knowledge and understanding by considering the photographs as evidence. By placing the photographs into a rich historical 'world', Hill ensures that students' substantive knowledge enables and strengthens their disciplinary understanding of the purposes behind and limitations of photographs in a particular context (Hill, 2024).

Conclusion

History curriculum planning presents a complex and daunting challenge for history teachers. The following principles can help support the curricular decisions made by leaders and teachers.

- Use curriculum time efficiently by planning for how one piece of knowledge accelerates another over time.
- Plan for world-building to help students build usable cognitive pictures of the past which are developed and compared over time.
- Plan for the layering of disciplinary knowledge across a curriculum by including concrete examples of the work of historians, encounters with evidence and the connections between the two.

CHAPTER B2
RESPONDING TO CHALLENGES IN HISTORY TEACHING THROUGH CURRICULUM PLANNING

The nature of history as a discipline brings particular challenges in curriculum planning and teaching, and may give rise to certain misconceptions. These often manifest most obviously at GCSE, when the huge volume of content in the current specifications places significant pressure on curriculum time. This can lead teachers and students to lose sight of the disciplinary dimensions of the subject. The best long-term solution to these problems is to pre-empt them with a rigorous and well-sequenced Key Stage 3. This allows misconceptions to be tackled early and thoroughly, and secure foundations to be laid before students tackle GCSE courses.

> See chapter B1.

Responding to the challenges of GCSE specifications
Problem 1: Amount of substantive knowledge
The selection and sequencing of knowledge is a profound challenge for history teachers. Historical knowledge is cumulative, meaning that planning a history curriculum is fundamentally different from curriculum planning in hierarchical subjects such as maths or science. Few individual pieces of knowledge are individually necessary, but the curriculum as a whole must be cumulatively sufficient in order to achieve the progress in students' knowledge and understanding envisioned by a department in its curricular aims, as discussed in Part A. History is an interpretative discipline and so history is always evolving. New scholarly approaches to source material bring with them new interpretations, and new demands on finite curriculum time.

> See chapters A5 and B1.

The current GCSE specifications present a different, but related, challenge because they require students to retain a large amount of detailed substantive knowledge. The challenge that this presents, particularly for students with lower eading

> Support for students with SEND in history lessons was called for in Ofsted's research review for history; see chapter A2.

ages or poor vocabulary knowledge and for students with some types of SEND, is a dominant consideration for teachers and subject leaders. Teachers routinely struggle to balance the pace of teaching required to cover the specification content against the need to review, recap and draw connections to ensure students have secure knowledge and recall of what they have learned.

While tightly managed course structures, careful attention to the specifications themselves and rigorous formative assessment can make a real difference, the most effective way to address this problem is by preparing students through a rich and rigorous Key Stage 3. This cannot, however, mean narrowing the curriculum, or the discipline, by directly teaching GCSE content or question types at Key Stage 3. Instead, careful planning for progression involves teaching content which enables subsequent learning, creating foundations of prior knowledge, substantive concepts and disciplinary knowledge which mean that students can approach the content of the GCSE course with greater confidence and fluency (Dickson, 2017).

See chapter A5.

Problem 2: Substantive concepts with shifting meaning

For students to develop a sophisticated understanding of the substantive content specified in many GCSE units, they need a secure understanding of certain powerful substantive concepts, as discussed in chapter A3. Common examples include 'communism' or 'revolution'. For example, explaining the unfolding political history of Weimar and Nazi Germany, a popular topic on several GCSE specifications, relies on students having an underlying understanding of the fear generated by communism in sections of German society in the 1930s. Substantive concepts shift in meaning across different historical (and contemporary) contexts, which makes them challenging to teach directly or at pace in a GCSE course. They are more securely understood where students have had multiple encounters with these concepts that serve as reference points for a deepening understanding (Counsell, 2017).

To provide the multiple encounters with key substantive concepts across multiple contexts needed for students to develop secure and flexible understanding of substantive concepts such as communism or revolution, planning for these encounters over the course of Key Stage 3 is again crucial

See chapter C3.

(Burnham and Brown, 2004; Ofsted, 2021). A student who has encountered communist ideas through an introduction to Karl Marx in an enquiry on the Industrial Revolution, and has deepened this in an exploration of Leninism in the context of the October Revolution in 1917, and again in an enquiry into similarity and difference in Soviet Russia and Nazi Germany, will have the well-developed schema needed to be able to understand and explain the role of communism in Weimar politics with some degree of sophistication.

Problem 3: Disciplinary misconceptions

Misconceptions about the nature of historical knowledge are well attested in research and can be exacerbated by the nature of GCSE assessment. Arthur Chapman found that students often come to the subject taking a 'naive empiricist' view that there is a fixed historical truth that was witnessed and is waiting to be discovered. He found that they can also be vulnerable to the opposing 'extreme postmodernist' position that no truth is possible and all interpretations are equally valid (Chapman, 2011). The danger of 'naive empiricism' is perhaps increased by the need to memorise 'facts' for use in exam questions, without opportunities to explore the evidential basis or contested interpretations of those 'facts'. Questions ostensibly about historical interpretations may also reinforce these misconceptions.

This problem can be addressed through cumulative encounters with source material from a range of different contexts and time periods, as well as through sequenced exposure to historians of different types and areas of expertise (Historical Association, 2019). Students who come with a highly developed understanding of the nature of historical truth-claims will also be better equipped to handle source and interpretations questions at GCSE.

See chapter A2 for the implications of using GCSE-style assessment at Key Stage 3.

Problem 4: Lack of usable mental models of the past

Students often find thematic studies at GCSE challenging owing to the chronological breadth of content they are required to study. Teachers may find that students are vulnerable to simplistic generalisations and misconceptions about the time periods they study, and at worst students may fall back on anachronistic or presentist assumptions.

See chapter A2.

The most effective solution to this problem lies, once again, at Key Stage 3 and is, again, an indirect one. Hill has theorised the importance of world-building in order to build rich cognitive pictures of the past in the minds of students (Hill, 2020). These provide the schemata of knowledge needed to underpin a thematic study at GCSE. A student equipped, by the end of Year 9, with a carefully cultivated mental model of medieval society, material culture, technology, weaponry, religious beliefs and structures of power will be much better able to assimilate new knowledge of the period, attending to complexity and nuance, when encountering the period again with a thematic focus and at pace.

See chapter B1.

Conclusion

Teaching history is challenging and teachers will continue to encounter these problems and others in the secondary classroom. Recognising that these problems are not inevitable, however, and that they can be addressed through carefully designed curricular sequencing, is critical. Continuous review and reflection on the effectiveness of the Key Stage 3 curriculum and its relationship to GCSE is required. Iterative curricular development over time is therefore one of the key drivers of success at GCSE and, most importantly, students' progression in history.

CHAPTER B3
CURRICULUM DESIGN IN PRACTICE

The curriculum outline shared in this chapter offers some concrete examples of how the principles discussed in the previous chapter might be followed in the history curriculum at a secondary school in England.

> This curriculum is not a model held up for imitation; rather it offers a concrete example for illustration and evaluation. It will be used as a reference throughout this book. The choice of GCSE and A-level topics is purely illustrative to show how Key Stage 3 relates to later years; these should not be regarded as a recommended programme of study.

See chapter A2 for discussion of changes to the national curriculum at Key Stage 3 over time.

Exemplar curriculum outline

Key Stage 3

50 hours teaching per school year, three one-hour lessons per fortnight. This curriculum uses enquiry questions taught over 4–6 lessons to frame most topics, but also makes use of short 'summary stories' lasting 1-2 lessons.

Year 7		Year 8		Year 9	
7a	How does Mary Beard use archaeological evidence to come to conclusions about the lives of people in Pompeii? [6]	8a	How does the historian Toby Green use oral histories to reach conclusions about West Africa? [5]	9a	What were the major changes of the 20th century? [2]
7b	Did the Normans bring a truckload of trouble? [3]	8b	What did 'colonisation' mean to the indigenous people of three places in the British Empire? [6]	9b	Why did the First World War break out? [3]
7c	How unlimited was the power of medieval monarchs? [5]	8c	How did the British transatlantic slave trade change the world? [4]	9c	How did different people experience the First World War? [6]

Year 7		Year 8		Year 9	
7d	Summary: Norman Sicily [1]	8d	What worlds was Josiah Wedgwood changing? [5]	9d	How did Russia become the world's first communist state? [4]
7e	Why did Alexios's empire survive? [5]	8e	What did 'revolution' mean in the Age of Revolutions? [6]	9e	Why did fascism flourish in Germany but not in Britain? [5]
7f	What does the story of Mansa Musa reveal about medieval Africa? [5]	8f	How did different people contribute to the abolition of the British transatlantic slave trade? [4]	9f	How does the historian Yasmin Khan use evidence to reach conclusions about experiences of the Second World War? [6]
7g	How did the Black Death change Walsham? [6]	8g	How typical was York's industrial revolution? [5]	9g	The Holocaust: a reflective investigation [6]
7h	How did Henry VII make Henry VIII so powerful? [3]	8h	Why was there no 'British Revolution' in the 1800s? [5]	9h	Was York's Cold War bunker really necessary? [5]
7i	How did the Reformation change life in Morebath? [5]	8i	Why did some women want to watch the world burn? [3]	9i	Women 1920–2020: would the Suffragettes have been satisfied? [4]
7j	What connected Elizabeth and the Elizabethans to wider worlds? [5]	8j	What do the people of Castle Leslie reveal about Ireland's 19th-century history? [5]	9j	How did British decolonisation change the world? [6]
7k	How did the 'world turn upside down' in the 17th century? [5]	8k	What was the experience for migrants to Britain, 1500 to 1914? [5]	9k	What was the experience for migrants to Britain, 1900 to 2000? [2]

▲ Figure B3.1: An example Key Stage 3 curriculum for discussion; by no means a 'model' or 'recommended' curriculum

Key Stage 4

Unit	Type of unit	Disciplinary emphasis
The People's Health, 1250–2000	Development study	Change and continuity
The Norman Conquest, 1060–1087	Depth study	Historical interpretations
History Around Us	Local site study of a ruined medieval abbey	Changes over time, significance, causation, using historical evidence
Living Under Nazi Rule, 1933–1945	Depth study	Using historical evidence
The Making of America, 1789–1900	Period study	Cause, consequence, diversity

▲ Figure B3.2: An example GCSE curriculum

Key Stage 5

Units/major topics	
The Earlier Tudors, 1485–1558	The reigns of Henry VII, Henry VIII, Edward VI and Mary I.
The Cold War in Asia, 1945–1993	The tensions of the Cold War as they played out in Japan, Korea, Vietnam, Cambodia and other areas of South-East Asia.
Civil Rights in the USA, 1865–1992	The changing position of African Americans, women, Native Americans and trade unions.
Personal Study	An independently researched essay.

▲ Figure B3.3: An example A-level curriculum

Looking under the bonnet

The curriculum outlined illustrates several of the ideas already discussed in chapters A3, A4 and B2 of this book.

Scope and selection of content • ──────── See chapters A4, A5 and B2.

In this example, the scope of the curriculum is extended by the decision to teach a larger number of shorter enquiries rather than structuring the curriculum around a single topic per half term. This allows for coverage of a broader range of substantive content. Notice how Year 7 expands well beyond the traditional topics of medieval England but does not entirely replace them. The Normans, Thomas Becket and the Black Death still appear, but they are complemented by studies of monarchy in the Byzantine Empire and Mali Empire, and of Norman Sicily.

This curriculum is inevitably still limited in scope: it could reasonably be criticised for its limited coverage of Middle Eastern or Chinese history, or of the Americas prior to or outside the scope of the British Empire. The wider curriculum of a school may play a role in decisions about scope: coverage of South America and of China in the geography curriculum, including with overt reference to the imperial history and legacy of South America, may go some way towards compensating for the absence of these histories in the Key Stage 3 history curriculum. *For further discussion of these curricular connections, see chapter B5.*

Coherence — *See chapter B2.*

Arguably, the number of topics covered in the curriculum outlined in this chapter presents a challenge to coherence, and risks leading to fragmentation in students' knowledge. The development of a coherent framework of knowledge is supported, however, by thematic and substantive threads running through the curriculum. One example is the way in which enquiries frequently return to the concept of 'revolution', as discussed in chapter A3. Figure B3.4 shows a small sample of other such threads.

	Units in which this theme features prominently
Power: monarchy, democracy, totalitarianism, protest	7e–f, 7h, 7j–k, 8e–f, 8h–i, 9a, 9d–e, 9g, 9i–j
Empire: colonialism, slavery, resistance	7b, 7d–f, 7j–k, 8b–g, 8j–k, 9a–d, f, 9j–k
Society: communities, class, ethnicity and race	7a–b, 7d, 7g, 7i, 8a–k, 9a, 9c–g, 9i–k

▲ Figure B3.4: Selected thematic and substantive threads revisited in the example curriculum shown in figure B3.1

Choosing some core themes, tracing them over time and 'making a fuss of them' in the teaching of these units can help to bring cohesion to a curriculum which, in the interests of scope, necessarily jumps between apparently diverse or disconnected topics.

> For further reading on the use of summary stories to build coherence, see Natalie Kesterton's article about using single-lesson narratives to bridge gaps at Key Stage 3 (Kesterton, 2019) and Jacob Olivey's article about using similar stories to plan a more diverse and coherent Year 7 curriculum (Olivey, 2021).

Rigour
See chapters A4 and B2.

Planning a rigorous history curriculum involves a finely-tuned balance: making the curriculum suitably challenging, in both substantive and disciplinary knowledge. Both substantive and disciplinary knowledge need to be simplified for students of history at secondary school; the history teacher's challenge lies in determining the appropriate and acceptable level of simplification. In this example curriculum, a greater number of 'shorter' enquiries of 4–5 lessons allows students to explore all the disciplinary concepts and encounter them in different ways. This enables teachers to plan for progression in disciplinary thinking across a single year. Thus, the curriculum is rigorously planned for the development of students' disciplinary knowledge.

Moreover, the curriculum incorporates enquiries in breadth, such as enquiry 8b into colonisation across different British Empire contexts, as well as enquiries in depth, for example investigating the Black Death in a single village. This makes the curriculum rigorous in the sense that it presents an appropriate level of challenge in the breadth and depth of substantive knowledge students must acquire and an acceptable simplification of the vast breadth of world history which does not unduly narrow students' knowledge to, for example, a single national story.

Finally, the enquiries are shaped by valid historical questions that are informed by recent scholarship, even if students do not directly encounter this scholarship in the classroom in every enquiry. Thus the curriculum consistently models to students how historians bring disciplinary lenses to bear on substantive knowledge of the past.

A curriculum can also be rigorous in its implementation at the level of individual lessons: the knowledge covered, the reading material used or the level of challenge in terms of disciplinary thinking. See chapter C3 for further exploration of some approaches in practice.

Sequencing • ──────────────────── See chapters B1 and B2.

The example Key Stage 3 curriculum outlined in this chapter is carefully sequenced so that it gradually expands students' schemata in relation to aspects of the past. Consider the opening enquiries in Year 7. After a look at Ancient Rome, students become acclimatised to the unfamiliar 11th century in the relatively familiar setting of England, building on nascent schemata students may already have as a result of studying the Anglo-Saxons and Vikings at primary school. It then lifts students' horizons to the Byzantine Empire but makes links to earlier learning through some familiar characters: students will be able to draw on prior knowledge about Christian monks and Norman knights to understand key characters in their study of Norman Sicily and the First Crusade. This carefully planned sequencing and coherence can help students to build a connected, cohesive imagined historical world.

Similarly, the curriculum coheres around certain geographical 'centres of gravity'. For example, India is introduced in 8b and reappears, in varying degrees of detail, in units 8g, 8i, 8k, 9b, 9c, 9f, 9j and 9k.

The careful sequencing extends beyond Key Stage 3, laying the foundations for later study. For example, in Units 8b, 8c and 8e students begin to explore the history of North America through the colonisation of indigenous nations, the transatlantic slave trade and the American Revolution. This prepares them for the GCSE Making of America course, which in turn provides the backstory for the Civil Rights in America unit at A-level.

Interplay of substantive and disciplinary knowledge • ──────── See chapter A3.

The interplay of substantive and disciplinary knowledge is planned for in a number of different ways in this curriculum. Units 7a and 8b and 9f exemplify how historians build knowledge and arrive at conclusions, as discussed in chapter B2. Some disciplinary concepts are explored intensively through a sequence of enquiries. Units 8c–8f all look at different facets of the concept of 'change' but in quite different ways, before 8g and 8h explore issues of continuity. This approach supports progression in students' thinking, as they build knowledge of different approaches historians take to change and continuity; it also highlights how the work of historians is shaped by the substantive content they study.

Diversification, decolonisation and world history ● ———— See chapter A4.

This curriculum incorporates diverse stories within traditional narratives, and also ensures that diverse global cultures and civilisations are taught in their own right. Consider how the enquiry on the First Crusade has been framed to focus on the Byzantine Empire and its challenges and call for support from Europe, rather than viewing events from the perspective of the Crusaders. Year 8 enquiries often begin with indigenous cultures – the Māori, Wampanoag, Akan and Mughals – before considering the impact of colonisation or transatlantic slavery. Unit 8a explores West African history by drawing on indigenous oral history traditions. Unit 9c explores experiences of fighting on different fronts, as well as the experience of soldiers of diverse nationalities fighting in Europe. In several enquiries, the 'British core' of content specified in the national curriculum is viewed from the perspective of outsiders: those who experienced the impact of British activity and policy around the world.

This chapter has drawn out several ways in which the example curriculum outlined early in the chapter exemplifies various principles and considerations for curriculum planning in history. Further reference will be made to this example curriculum in subsequent chapters.

CHAPTER B4
CORE AND HINTERLAND KNOWLEDGE

Distinguishing between 'core' and 'hinterland' knowledge, as discussed in chapter A3, can help curriculum designers and teachers of history to navigate the contested selection of curriculum content and to consider the functions of different forms of knowledge. 'Core' content is that which we aim for students to take away from our lessons – the 'residue' of their encounters with substantive knowledge, or as Christine Counsell (2018) describes it, 'the things that can be captured as proposition'. 'Hinterland' is the contextual or background detail in which the core is embedded and through which it acquires shape and meaning.

See chapter A2 for developments in history education relating to substantive knowledge. See chapter A3 for an introduction to core and hinterland, and signposts to wider reading. The implications of core and hinterland for progression are also considered in chapter A5.

While it can be tempting to reduce our curriculum, resources and explanations to the core knowledge that we want students to take away, this will ultimately be counterproductive. As Josh Vallance (2021) writes:

> 'Simply drilling students on core knowledge would reduce the curriculum to the memorisation of facts. It would amount to a mutilation of our craft and a disservice to our children. And not simply because the mechanics of this would likely be dry and lifeless, but because the knowledge students leave with would be fundamentally shallow.'

Jonathan Grande (2022) explains the fundamental nature of the relationship between core and hinterland in this way:

> 'The hinterland knowledge, then, is crucial. And it needs to be carefully selected, planned and positioned in an enquiry. Debated and discussed and curated by members of a department. It cannot be taken for granted. Left for an individual teacher to decide or find. Or sacrificed in an ill-guided attempt to reach the core knowledge more quickly…miss out the story – miss out the hinterland – and there can be no residue. There can be no core.'

Using hinterland to teach the core

Rich, layered and intentional hinterland detail can enable students to reach and take away a residual 'core' understanding. There are many ways to do this and story can be one vehicle for it. Hugh Richards took this approach for the Nazi Germany GCSE course. These stories (figures B4.1 and B4.2) focus on specific individuals whose lives illuminate, and render human, concrete and memorable, the wider picture of events in the period.

Marinus van der Lubbe

In February 1933, the streets of Berlin were, in some ways, very cold. As he walked, Marinus van der Lubbe pulled his jacket collar tighter, shielding his neck from the icy night air. He leant into the bitter wind, shifting the heavy bag from one shoulder to the other. He skirted the homeless men who huddled into the sides of buildings. If they survived the night, they would continue to trudge these streets looking for work or queuing for a handout of warm, thin stew and a scrap of bread. Perhaps Marinus' plan would help them. Perhaps he could spark the change they so desperately needed. In other ways, Berlin's streets were dangerously hot. Since the Depression had begun, politics and many elections had not just caused heated arguments about Germany's future. Back in 1931, when van der Lubbe was last in Berlin, he had been impressed by the street violence between the political groups.

▲ Figure B4.1: Extract from a story about late Weimar Germany

The aim of this story is that students retain a secure core understanding of the dangerous, divided social and political atmosphere of late Weimar Germany. This is achieved through the fine personal details of van der Lubbe's story. For example, the description of the material conditions that van der Lubbe experiences and sees on the streets of Berlin make it easy for students to infer his motivation for supporting communism, as well as the motivations of Germans who had turned their support to the Nazis or communists. The mention of van der Lubbe's experience of political violence also contributes to the wider mental picture of danger and disorder that students are building. This again helps to explain the political choices made by German people, and the divisions that developed in the country.

Georg Elser

In 1938, Elser refused to salute the Nazi parade passing through his town, Königsbronn. It was risky, but Georg Elser was prepared to take risks. Soon after this he went to Munich to observe the Nazis' annual celebration of the 1923 Putsch at the Bürgerbräukeller beer hall, from where Hitler, Röhm and the old generals had marched. Of course, nobody mentioned Röhm any more. Elser wanted this place to be remembered for a very different reason. There was no question of trusting others to help. Any conversation could be overheard. Regular visits to his house by anyone new would be spotted by his block leader. Questions asked. Anyone could turn him over to the merciless, black-gloved hands of the Gestapo. He worked alone, throughout 1938.

First, a new job at an armament factory, back in Königsbronn. There were many armament factories these days. He stole gunpowder and fuses. Then a second job, at Vollmer quarry, where he stole more explosives and detonators. He bought metal parts from the Niederholer locksmiths. Elser taught himself, exploding prototype bombs in nearby fields. It had to work first time. This target wouldn't give him a second chance.

▲ Figure B4.2: Extract from a story about resistance to the Nazis

The aim of this story is that students retain a core understanding of the power of the Nazi police state and how difficult it was to resist. This is made vivid and personal through Elser's fear of being turned in to the Gestapo and, more indirectly, through his obsessively careful preparation. By detailing how difficult it was to steal the objects Elser needed without detection, the story also indirectly helps to explain why others chose not to undergo the same risks and therefore did not oppose the Nazi regime. Glancing references to the Munich Putsch and to Ernst Röhm help students connect this story to their broader developing narrative of the Nazi Party in the 1920s and 1930s. These also reinforce the core understanding by demonstrating how the Nazi Party memorialised its own history to legitimate its control of Germany, and how any internal enemies were purged and that history ruthlessly rewritten.

The relationship between core and hinterland is a fundamental one and functions within lessons, units and across a curriculum as a whole. While much of the rich hinterland knowledge students encounter will ultimately be forgotten, it is only through the hinterland that students can reach the core takeaways of a curriculum (Grande, 2023).

CHAPTER B5
CONNECTING TO OTHER SUBJECTS

As we saw in chapter A3, there is an important distinction to be made between the academic discipline of history and the subject of history in schools, but school history still needs to retain its disciplinary identity. However, it is also true that well-planned interdisciplinarity can be very powerful. Kenneth Nordgren (2021) suggests that 'subject education does not contradict cross-curricular and interdisciplinary activities, and in order to understand the production of new knowledge it is important to learn to work across borders'. Drawing inspiration from Nordgren, Rachel Lewin (2022) outlines the following guiding ideas for interdisciplinarity with integrity.

- Intelligent interdisciplinarity grows out of disciplinary thinking and does not distort subject integrity.
- Intelligent interdisciplinarity can be built through big-picture thinking or small-scale collaboration with colleagues.
- Intelligent interdisciplinarity can consolidate and deepen understanding of substantive concepts.

This chapter will exemplify ways in which these guiding ideas can be put into practice, and how interdisciplinarity can enhance students' experience of history, in a range of ways.

Providing enabling context

History teachers can work with teachers from other disciplines to consider the mutually enabling power of what they teach. Lewin (2022) takes a similar approach, intentionally designing her Russian Revolution unit to revolve around substantive concepts such as communism, capitalism, inequality and oppression, which will later prove helpful when studying *Animal Farm* in English. In a similar way, Hugh Richards has collaborated with the head of geography in his school to ensure that British colonialism in India is taught prior to a case study on modern India in the geography curriculum. Such collaboration can ensure the intentional layering of knowledge across subject disciplines. Knowledge that is deployed in multiple and complementary contexts in this way can become more generative, fertile and flexible.

Filling substantive gaps ⎯⎯⎯⎯⎯⎯⎯⎯⎯⎯⎯ See chapter B3.

History teachers can also consider the broader diet of substantive knowledge that students encounter in other subjects and use that to help inform curricular decisions. The curriculum outlined in chapter B3 does not include any specific focus on South American history. This could be mitigated through collaboration with the geography department, who might teach the consequences of Spanish colonisation, for example as part of a unit on development. Similarly, in Elizabeth Carr's department, there is limited time in the curriculum for Chinese history, with brief encounters during enquiries on the Mongol Empire and British Empire; however, China and its recent development and worldwide economic influence is an important case study running through the geography curriculum at Key Stage 3. Moreover, what students learn in the geography curriculum about China's growing influence in some African countries complements students' learning in history about colonisation and decolonisation in Africa.

Disciplinary non-examples or revisiting with a new disciplinary lens

It can also be fruitful to make the boundaries between subject disciplines explicit to students. A history teacher might seek to make the unique status of historical knowledge explicit to students by explaining that historical knowledge is necessarily different from and more provisional than knowledge in science, in part because historians do not have direct access to the past (Ashbee, 2021).

Revisiting the same resources or texts through different subject lenses also creates an opportunity to highlight disciplinary distinctiveness, while consolidating and layering substantive knowledge. An English teacher might teach a unit on *Oliver Twist* which explores the literary techniques, characters and plot of the novel. A history teacher in the same school might then revisit extracts from the book as evidence in an enquiry into the experience of different groups during the Industrial Revolution. Encountering the same text in these two contexts could help to illustrate the disciplinary distinctiveness of each subject, as well as the connections between them. Similarly, Mary Woolley used

Thomas Hardy's *The Withered Arm* as evidence in an enquiry on change and continuity in the period 1750–1900 and found that literature had the potential to build a richer, more detailed context for her students (Woolley, 2003).

Environmental history and interdisciplinarity

Teaching climate change also seems to pose a 'challenge to subject-bound curricula' (Hawkey, 2023). Seeking to do justice to environmental history in a school curriculum can, however, offer opportunities for intelligent interdisciplinarity, inspired by the ways in which environmental historians also reach across subject boundaries. Paula Worth made evidence the focus of an enquiry comparing and contrasting the types of sources used by environmental historians to learn about changes to the flora, fauna and landscape of England with the types of sources historians have used to study other phenomena (Hawkey et al., 2024). Students are thereby left with a richer and more expansive understanding of the subject and its boundaries.

Part C

CHAPTER C1
WHAT IS AND ISN'T INSTRUCTIONAL TEACHING IN THE HISTORY CLASSROOM?

What is instructional teaching?

Over the past few years, teachers and researchers have increasingly advocated for instructional teaching. This approach emphasises the role of the teacher in explicitly directing and structuring student learning (Rosenshine, 2012). History teachers must carefully navigate several tensions when adopting an instructional approach. This section will explore and exemplify how this can be achieved while remaining true to history's disciplinary structures.

WalkThrus

Models exist to support teachers to consider and practise instructional teaching; one such model is WalkThrus. WalkThrus model a range of effective teaching techniques which have been compiled from educational research. Each technique is broken down into five steps, accompanied by a visual guide. Teachers make use of the steps to consider a teaching technique in detail before practising the technique. Following practice, teachers consider which aspects of the technique they do well and which they might need to emphasise.

> WalkThrus have been created and developed by Tom Sherrington and Oliver Caviglioli. For full details see the WalkThrus site: www.walkthrus.co.uk.

While it is not essential to make use of a model to attempt instructional teaching, this approach has certain advantages. A model such as WalkThrus allows teachers to create and use a shared language when discussing and evaluating a technique. Instructional models also facilitate a shared understanding of how to use a technique well through the common reference points (the five steps), which allow teachers to engage with the same ideas, in the same manner.

Although the teaching techniques in WalkThrus are not subject-specific, the model is designed to be adapted so that teachers consider the implementation of the five steps in the context of their own subject. Parts of each WalkThru may be more or less relevant in a particular subject, or for a particular class or topic, but the model offers flexibility by encouraging teachers to consider this and to adapt each WalkThru to their context before putting the techniques into practice.

Themes

This section explores three areas in which the application of generic pedagogical approaches or models, such as WalkThrus, might be in tension with the principles of great history teaching, or might be challenging to reconcile with history's disciplinary structures and forms of accounting.

Each theme discussed in this section is further exemplified by discussion of a WalkThru and how it might be used in a history classroom (Figures C1.1, C1.3 and C1.4).

Theme 1: Instructional teaching in history is rich in story and cultivates curiosity

The emphasis on instructional teaching has brought with it a reclamation of teacher talk and explanation. The importance of precise, layered explanations which skilfully combine abstract concepts and concrete examples remains central to great teaching of history. Storytelling in the classroom has also attracted renewed attention. If learning is a change in long-term memory (and, per Willingham (2009), 'memory is the residue of thought') then how teachers talk and how they design texts they use in the classroom plays a vital role in cultivating students' curiosity as well as maintaining clarity. This is particularly important in history because the construction of analytical arguments, and engagement with complex and sometimes contradictory evidence and interpretations, is central to the discipline.

> Daniel Willingham's (2009) maxim, 'memory is the residue of thought', encapsulates the principle that students learn by thinking, because they remember what they think about. Thinking is therefore a much better – though less visible – indicator of learning than other proxies such as finishing tasks.

> **Example 1**
>
> Ms Stewart is teaching the causes of the First World War. She plans to begin with an extended verbal explanation of the causes of increased tension and the importance of nationalism, militarism and imperialism. The explanation spans from the launch of HMS *Dreadnought* in 1906 to the outbreak of war.

> **Example 2**
>
> Ms Stewart is teaching the causes of the First World War. She structures the lesson around a carefully designed text which provides a narrative of the events leading up to the First World War. Ms Stewart carefully plans where in the text she will ask students to speculate on later events or introduce illustrative examples, maps or images. She pauses and uses mini-whiteboards to check the understanding of the whole class as they read the narrative together.

The teacher in example 2 demonstrates a number of important traits of instructional teaching in history. First, she is carefully directing the way that students are engaged in the narrative she presents, using student prediction and generative questions to cultivate their curiosity. While this might not initially appear the most direct method of teaching the narrative, it helps to ensure that students are thinking deeply. This is in contrast to the teacher in example 1, who did not check whether her students were thinking deeply at any point during the explanation or hold them to account for doing so. The teacher in example 2 has also directed students to maps and images as a means to build rich cognitive pictures of the past and mental maps of the spaces important to the narrative. Mike Hill has written about the importance of world-building in order to immerse students in the period of study (Hill, 2020).

> On world-building, see also chapter B2.

Five steps	How to adapt/what to consider in the history classroom
likely to be a useful routine approach	There are many ways to use texts with students in the history classroom, but they are not all appropriate for every topic or activity, or at any stage in an enquiry. For example, a class might benefit from teacher-led whole-class reading at the start of an enquiry, or with a complex text. Alternatively a teacher might start by reading aloud and then make use or choral or paired reading once students are more familiar with the text. Text is central to history's forms of accounting so reading should be across the curriculum. Until students are familiar with how to read and the form different texts take, teacher-led whole-class reading is likely to be a useful routine approach *(See also chapters A3 and C4.)*
2. Annotate and practise	This is essential. Thought needs to be given to what to stress, which words or phrases might need unpacking, where prior knowledge could be recalled to help students to make sense of the text being used, and how to emphasise the most important knowledge and ideas for students to take away.
3. Express and stress	This step is also important to consider. The pre-teaching of vocabulary can have pitfalls: while it might seem that this will make a text more accessible to students, words and phrases are most effectively taught and learned in context, rather than decontextualised.
4. Chunk and stop	This step can be planned along with annotate and practise (step 2).
5. Establish the gist	This is an important feature of using text in history lessons: students need to understand how new knowledge relates to the topic being learned, but also how this is building their wider historical understanding. For example, if academic historical scholarship is used in lessons, the text should be integral to curricular planning, rather than used incidentally to add colour or additional challenge (Jenner, 2019; Ofsted, 2021).

▲ Figure C1.1: Whole-class reading routines (*Teaching WalkThrus* Book 2, pp. 78–79)

Theme 2: Instructional teaching in history supports students with effective scaffolding

Instructional teaching emphasises structure and explicit modelling in order to ensure that students succeed. It also gives them space to make meaning and has the ultimate goal of student independence. Research into metacognition has shown the importance of fading scaffolding over time so that students become independent (Education Endowment Foundation, 2020). It is crucial for teachers to manage this tension effectively so that students engage in authentic historical reasoning.

Spider planning (figure C1.2) is one example of an approach which manages this tension flexibly and effectively. It is a visual essay-planning format which supports students to link their planning and writing to the conceptual focus of a question and scaffolds structural decisions and the selection of examples. The spider plan can be used slowly and in a carefully structured way when knowledge is less familiar, or students are less fluent and a more directive approach is needed. It can also be used with little or no guidance at later stages when fluency, knowledge and confidence have developed.

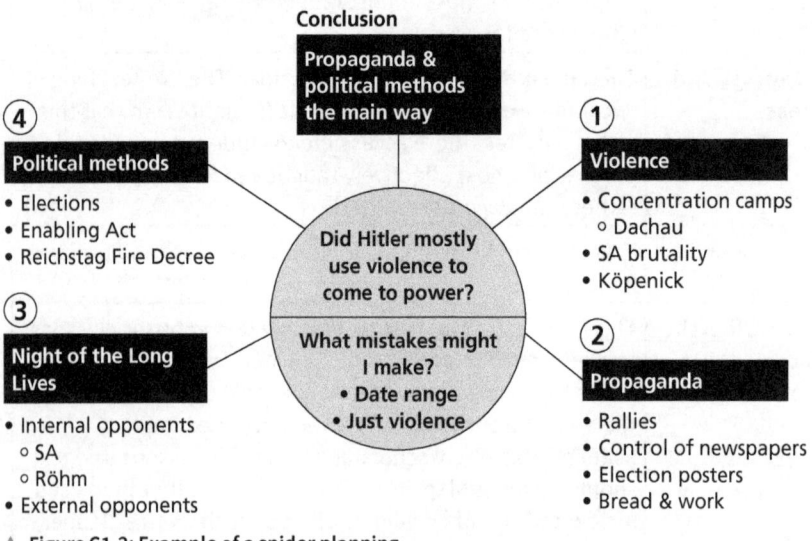

▲ Figure C1.2: Example of a spider planning

Another approach that can help students to build independence over time is an 'Apollo 13 test'. Inspired by the engineering innovations made during the Apollo 13 crisis, this approach asks students to plan a piece of writing or engage in a task using only a pen and a piece of paper in order to build independence and fluency.

If every process or task is explicitly modelled for students, this can leave little space for them to engage in historical thinking or reasoning for themselves. This is particularly true in relation to the construction of knowledge in the subject, and without space to reach their own conclusions students cannot be said to have engaged in meaningful evidential thinking.

Example 1
Mr Clark puts a cartoon about the Nazi–Soviet Pact on the board. He annotates the source with details from the cartoon as well as analysis of the source's provenance. Students listen and copy down what the teacher writes on the board.

Example 2
Mr Clark gives students a copy of a cartoon about the Nazi–Soviet Pact and asks them to annotate it completely independently, analysing details from the source and its provenance. He provides no frame or support.

In example 1 the students have no space to make meaning. In example 2, however, students are given plenty of space to make meaning, but the quality of their work and learning may be low as a result of insufficient knowledge and guidance; this will depend upon the nature of their prior knowledge and experience. A history teacher must manage tasks, lessons and the curriculum carefully to ensure the right amount of space to make meaning is given to students at the right time.

Five steps	How to adapt/ what to consider in the history classroom
1. Activate prior knowledge with a retrieval activity	The knowledge and understanding being retrieved should be relevant to the lesson, and this should be made explicit to students. Elsewhere in this book we explore the importance of sequencing for creating a coherent curriculum; emplotment of topics should be intentional and will provide opportunities to affirm, disrupt and expand students' prior learning. Theme 3 (instructional teaching in history is attentive to knowledge) will further explore principles for effective retrieval practice in the history classroom.
2. Invite students to make predictions	If students are asked to make predictions, the questions history teachers ask need to be carefully phrased. History lessons should not become guessing games relying on students' presentist assumptions. Rather, students could be encouraged to use prior knowledge, alongside contextual understanding of the current topic, to predict, for example, consequences, or similarities and differences. Students might recall their knowledge of the French Revolution and be asked to use this to make predictions about the nature or course of the Russian Revolution and how it might resemble or differ from events in France.
3. Verify the predictions	If a history teacher chooses to use this technique, this step is vital! Students can easily and quickly confuse fact and fiction when studying the past. If this happens, or if misconceptions go unchecked, students will have a very distorted understanding of the topic in question.
4. Explore incorrect predictions	It is critical at this step to establish the facts – incorrect predictions need not be entertained or laboured. The purpose of step 2, considering the example given in this table, would be to develop students' understanding of the substantive concept of revolution. Students' thoughts on the nature of revolution in France, alongside their contextual understanding of pre-1905 or 1917 Russia, would help them to make more sense of how revolution unfolded in Russia. The purpose of this step is not to entertain a 'what if?' version of history.

Five steps	How to adapt/ what to consider in the history classroom
5. Reinforce and revisit	To support this step, and considering the example given of retrieval related to a substantive concept, history teachers might wish to make use of a framework to allow students to develop their understanding of 'revolution'.

▲ Figure C1.3: How aspects of the WalkThru 'Predict & verify', might be used in the history classroom (adapted from *Teaching WalkThrus 3*, pp. 88–89)

Theme 3: Instructional teaching in history is attentive to knowledge

Instructional teaching emphasises the importance of knowledge retention over time. Students need to engage in retrieval so that knowledge is increasingly committed to long-term memory because knowledge changes what they are able to see and think when they encounter new knowledge. Teachers can manage the layering of knowledge over time by skilfully retrieving prior knowledge at just the right time to support an encounter with new knowledge and create the connections that form secure schemata. Instructional teaching in history must pay careful attention to knowledge without adopting approaches which work against a clear understanding of the subject.

An increasingly popular approach in recent years has been to ask students to engage in retrieval tasks at the start of a lesson. While retrieval opportunities can be very powerful for students, it is critical that the instructional history teacher does not reduce historical thinking and understanding to simple questions and answers. While being attentive to knowledge, the instructional history teacher could keep the following principles in mind.

- Connectivity: ensure that retrieval opportunities, and classroom tasks in general, are not structured around isolated facts but support students in connecting and integrating what they have learned into meaningful patterns and categories.
- Coherence: consider the connections between every lesson, task and question and the curriculum as a whole. Use this to guide classroom decision making.
- Constant reference to enquiry questions as the driving force for student learning is very useful in implementing both of the preceding principles across a lesson or enquiry.

These principles are exemplified in figure C1.4.

Five steps	How to adapt/ what to consider in the history classroom
1. Establish the core	Core and hinterland are both crucial for building historical understanding, but have different roles. Of course, the core needs to be established because that is the knowledge students should take away from the lesson, but we would not want to emphasise this at the expense of hinterland. Use of frameworks in history lessons can support students to recognise what content is core. (see also chapter A3).
2. Map out the hinterland in broad terms	Hinterland fosters students' sense of period and historical perspective, and in this way it contributes to a broader historical understanding. This should not, however, be confused with furnishing students with extraneous detail relating to the period or topic (such as biographical detail or a series of contemporaneous events). Hinterland must be intentional and address a gap in students' understanding. The first and second steps in this WalkThru might be reversed in a history lesson. Stating the core before students have hinterland knowledge can risk presenting a reductive interpretation of the past.
3. Plan hinterland reference as context for the core	This step is essential. Hinterland needs to be used explicitly and intentionally to help students to make meaning of the core. Grande (2022) has written in detail about how history teachers can do this.
4. Engage students in hinterland research tasks	This may or may not have a useful role when teaching secondary history. If practised, this step would require careful scaffolding from the teacher. As mentioned in the WalkThru, 'meanwhile elsewhere' tasks could be useful for this step, but teacher curation of these resources can support students to acquire meaningful hinterland knowledge.
5. Adopt a responsive organic approach	Students benefit from passionate and well-informed history teachers, but as mentioned, hinterland needs to be used explicitly and intentionally to help students to make meaning of the core.

▲ Figure C1.4: How aspects of the WalkThru 'Deliver core; signpost hinterland' might be used in the history classroom (adapted from *Teaching WalkThrus 1*, pp. 64–65)

The 'meanwhile elsewhere' resources were developed by Will Bailey-Watson and Richard Kennett. They can be accessed via the 'meanwhile elsewhere' website: www.meanwhileelsewhereinhistory.wordpress.com. Bailey-Watson and Kennett (2019) have also written about this project in *Teaching History*.

Conclusions and cautions

Instructional teaching is an approach with great potential and power, but it needs to be considered and deployed with care. Generic techniques to support instructional teaching can be useful ways to build shared understanding, however:

- as in the case of WalkThrus, generic techniques should be evidence-informed;
- generic teaching techniques should be used with fidelity to the nature of the subject.

Instructional teaching must be approached with the subject foremost in a teacher's mind if its potential is to be realised. This will ensure that generic pedagogical approaches do not distort or overwhelm the subject. For consideration of how to reconcile generic and subject-specific approaches see Sherrington (2023).

CHAPTER C2
HOW CAN STUDENTS BE GIVEN SPACE TO EXPLORE AND MAKE MEANING?

Structured and instructional approaches, as explored elsewhere in this book, often work very well for teaching history. It is also important, however, to give students opportunities to explore more independently and to make meaning for themselves. This is sometimes called mode B teaching (Sherrington and Caviglioli, 2020). Giving this space to students is particularly important in history because it helps to cultivate their relationship with historical knowledge. We could not meaningfully say that students had learned the subject if they had never had the chance to form an argument or to wrestle with an historical question for themselves. Giving students the space to make meaning can happen at every level, from moment-to-moment pedagogy all the way through to unit and curriculum planning. Planning to do this successfully requires careful attention to the layers of knowledge and understanding that students have accumulated at a particular point, as well as intentional cultivation of their curiosity and desire to explore.

Making pedagogical space for meaning making

Students can be given the opportunity to make meaning through the moment-to-moment decisions that a teacher makes in the classroom. Consider the following examples:

Example 1
Mrs Annan gives a verbal explanation of Hitler's actions between 1935 and the outbreak of the Second World War. She structures the explanation clearly and uses maps on the board to differentiate the steps as well as the logic of each action.

Example 2

Mrs Annan gives an explanation of Hitler's actions between 1935 and the outbreak of the Second World War using maps on the board. She pauses after explaining Hitler's reoccupation of the Rhineland in 1936 and asks the class, 'What options do Britain, France and other countries have? What are the problems with those actions? Answer on your whiteboards.' Later, after explaining the Nazi–Soviet Pact, Mrs Annan asks the class, 'What do you predict will happen next? Write your ideas on your whiteboards.' Finally, she asks, 'Do you think that appeasement or the actions of Hitler was the most important factor behind these events? Write your judgements on your whiteboard and be ready to defend your position.'

In example 2, the teacher gives the students space to predict, explain and make judgements about the history they are learning. This supports the students to be cognitively active during the explanation, increasing the likelihood that they will remember the substantive content explained to them. In relation to understanding the nature of history as a discipline, this approach reinforces the contingent nature of historical events, and the provisional, constructed nature of historical knowledge.

The crucial consideration here is that these pedagogical decisions accumulate. If a student only ever receives a diet that is similar to example 1 then they have little room to explore. If a teacher sensitively and responsively integrates opportunities for independent reasoning in response to fertile questions, these will accumulate into a very different and more meaningful learning experience.

Designing tasks and units which provide space to explore

Teachers can also provide students with tasks and units that give them space to explore. These must be planned carefully so this space is provided with enough structure and at the right time. Chloe Bateman (2018) designed a unit which culminated in students writing their own historical fiction about life in medieval England. This unit was carefully designed to build necessary substantive knowledge, as well as reading and analysing the writing of historical scholarship that would later empower students to write in a historically accurate way that was sensitive to the period.

The Covid-19 pandemic also prompted some history teachers to consider meaningful independent learning. Rachel Lewin (2023) used curated research materials on an online platform to allow her students on the Isles of Scilly to explore how migration has shaped modern Britain. This sequence culminated in students curating their own objects for a local migration exhibit. It is an excellent example of the way in which authentic outcomes can act as a driver and provide structure when giving students more independence.

There is also a place for historically grounded drama and role play in the classroom, when this is carefully directed by the teacher with a pedagogical purpose to develop substantive or disciplinary knowledge (Luff, 2000; 2001; 2003; 2023; Moorhouse, 2009; Kerridge, 2017).

See chapter D1.

Trips, visits and other opportunities for exploration

Trips and visits can also provide students with valuable chances to encounter the past in an authentic and exploratory way; proper structure and planning are again vital. Planning a First World War battlefields trip, Hugh Richards identified the need to strike a balance between explicit teaching and opportunities for students to explore the site for themselves. Explicit teaching is needed before and during the trip in order to allow students to understand and interpret what they see, while opportunities for students to explore sites for themselves build on these foundations of knowledge. Richards identified personal and local connections as well as memorialisation as appropriate ways to grant agency to students in this context. These also offered opportunities for students to undertake research before or after the trip itself (Richards, 2023).

Visiting museums, archives or historic sites or inviting archivists, historians or curators into school can also provide students with authentic encounters with historical knowledge, evidence and argument as well as a chance to explore the subject in a new way. Having the chance to see or touch a physical object alongside considering it as evidence can help reinforce the concrete nature of the past and make the subject more tangible. Providers such as the National Archives are experts in giving students the chance to engage with evidence in a way that is more open than it would be in a classroom setting.

CHAPTER C3
EXAMPLE LESSONS

This chapter provides some practical examples of history lessons, exemplifying the ideas explored in the previous two chapters. It presents individual lessons from the example in chapter B3. The lesson outlines below assume one hour per lesson. They do not explain adaptations to the needs of students with SEND; teachers should make these to meet the specific needs of individuals in a particular class. An outline of each lesson is followed by a brief analysis highlighting ways in which these lessons exemplify the thinking in other areas of the book. These links are identified in square brackets.

In particular, the lessons illustrate instructional teaching in history, as discussed in chapter C1. The lesson examples show teachers:

- introducing new enquiries
- telling stories
- guiding discussion of sources
- questioning students, using questions that target specific substantive and disciplinary takeaways.

These elements are highlighted in the commentary after specific lessons.

Key Stage 3 lessons

These example lessons are drawn from the Year 9 curriculum outlined in chapter B3.

Enquiry about fascism in the 20th century

This enquiry explores the nature of fascism by comparing German and British examples. Students learn about how differing contexts produced differing outcomes and how these outcomes resulted from the particular combination of causal factors rather than from a single cause.

> These Key Stage 3 examples are taken from enquiries. See chapter A3 for the use of enquiry questions and chapter A2 for developments in the use of enquiry in history teaching.

Enquiry question: Why did fascism flourish in Germany but not in Britain?	
Builds on knowledge of the outcomes of the First World War and disciplinary work on causes of the First World War	Builds towards Year 9 Second World War unit, GCSE Nazi Germany course and further exploration of causation

Purpose of lesson and desired takeaways	Teacher	Students
Lesson 1: Introduces concept and key context. **Takeaways:** 1. What fascism was in the 1920s and 1930s, to support GCSE Nazi Germany course. 2. The conditions necessary for fascism to flourish, and why these often need to be part of causal arguments. 3. The First World War and the Great Depression affected Britain and Germany differently.	Introduces enquiry and ties it into previous learning. Explains what fascism was, invites questions and uses questioning to check for understanding. Poses key question: How desperate were the people of Germany and Britain by 1932? Poses key question: Why was Germany more seriously affected than Britain? Sets the scene for Hitler's rise with some storytelling about him as an electoral force.	Note down key aspects from teacher's explanation, using a series of guided headings. Annotate information about impact of the First World War and the Depression to draw out differences between countries. Have short, paired discussions and feedback to class.
Lesson 2: Explores Hitler's rise to power, using a structured narrative followed by an exploration of the case study of a single German town, Northeim (Lacey and Shepherd, 1997).		

Purpose of lesson and desired takeaways	Teacher	Students
Lesson 3: Uses British context to offer a contrasting situation. **Takeaways:** Fascism failed to gain popularity in Britain. This was due to a post-war context, weaker leadership, economic situation and national identity that was different to Germany's. Different causal conditions, even if superficially similar, produce different outcomes.	After recall task, leads questioning about a photo of Oswald Mosley, asking students to suggest where and when it was taken. Leads reading of narrative about rise of British fascism. Uses documentary and original newsreel footage to explore the 'Battle of Cable Street' with questioning. Uses questioning and class discussion to clarify, correct and consolidate paired thinking. Reads/projects some of the answers and discusses with the class the reasoning expressed, providing feedback in preparation for outcome task.	Recall key conditions needed for fascism to flourish, knowledge from lesson 1, then discuss photo as prompted by teacher. Pick out similarities and differences to Germany from narrative. Take a few notes about Cable Street, focusing on inferring reasons why fascism failed in Britain. Complete analysis grid in pairs to compare conditions in Britain and Germany. Write short paragraph that explores the reasons for differing outcomes in Britain and Germany, reaching and expressing their own judgements about the key factor that 'made the difference' in Germany and why.
Lesson 4: Card sort task followed by a short written outcome task in which students identify and explain which factor(s) 'made the difference' in Germany.		

▲ **Figure C3.1:** Example of a four-lesson enquiry for Year 9

Things to notice

1. The key substantive takeaways are the driving focus of the unit, so lessons 1–3 build detailed substantive knowledge of Britain and Germany during the period, with a tight focus on the enquiry question to guide the selection of substantive knowledge and how students think about and use it. This substantive knowledge lays the foundations for the study of Weimar and Nazi Germany at GCSE. [A4 & B1]
2. A tight focus on the enquiry question in each lesson ensures that substantive knowledge is taught through a disciplinary lens: in this case, a causal lens. Identifying the 'factor that made the difference' trains students in a frequently deployed mode of causal reasoning, which they will subsequently use in essay questions at GCSE and A-level. [A3]
3. Recall activities focus on the substantive knowledge that will be most useful in the enquiry outcome and the lesson that follows. [B1 & B2]
4. A writing activity provides an opportunity to practise an aspect of disciplinary writing, as part of the learning process rather than with the primary purpose of assessment. [C5]

Enquiry focusing on the work of historian Yasmin Khan

The enquiry question looks at varied experiences of the Second World War and the methods of an historian, challenging Year 9 students to consider how a historian studies those varied experiences and forms and interpretation on the basis of evidence. Here are lessons 1, 2 and 3 of that enquiry:

Enquiry question: How does the historian Yasmin Khan use evidence to reach conclusions about experiences of the Second World War?	
Builds on prior knowledge of India built though an enquiry on Mughal India.	Builds towards exploration of Partition through the lens of decolonisation.

Purpose of lesson and desired takeaways	Teacher	Students
Lesson 1: Why did Mohammed Khan go to war? This lesson builds substantive knowledge of India during the Second World War through the case study of one solider. Students consider and prioritise the possible motivations of soldiers signing up to the Indian Volunteer Army.		
Lesson 2: What does Yasmin Khan say about experiences of the Second World War? **Takeaways:** Interpretations are based on carefully selected source material. Trying to find out about India during the Second World War means the sources that can be drawn upon as evidence are different from those available for other times and places. Yasmin Khan is a historian with particular interests and who is asking particular questions. This is true of all historians. India during the Second World War was a complex place and was shaped by the First World War as well as by independence movements.	Introduces enquiry and ties it to previous learning. Introduces Yasmin Khan through a video addressing the students. Reads two extracts from Yasmin Khan's book *The Raj at War*. Checks comprehension through cold-calling and models and scaffolds analysis of the extracts for students. Questions students and facilitates class discussion to clarify, correct and consolidate understanding of the remaining passages.	Watch the video and write a list of facts about Yasmin Khan. Highlight the key arguments in each extract, guided by modelling. Analyse four further extracts with greater independence. Use the examples sheet to suggest sources of evidence on which Yasmin Khan may have drawn in the extracts they have read. Watch video of Yasmin Khan discussing the source material that she actually used. Check and assess their answers from the previous task.

Purpose of lesson and desired takeaways	Teacher	Students
	Explains the possible sources of evidence that Yasmin Khan's interpretation might have been based on. Models to students how to infer possible sources from Yasmin Khan's text.	
Lesson 3: Was the Indian Army truly voluntary? **Takeaways:** Historians often encounter problems with the source material that they have available. They can address this issue by reading evidence in a way that it was not intended to be read and/or seek out different sources of evidence. The choices and incentives facing prospective soldiers in the Indian Army were complex and this makes judgements difficult.	Sets up recall task on the reasons soldiers joined the Indian Volunteer Army. Introduces video of Yasmin Khan talking about the problem of finding out whether the Indian Army was truly voluntary. Introduces source material that might help answer the question of whether the Indian Army was voluntary. Models the placement of one source on the spectrum. Uses questioning and class discussion to draw out a range of students' judgements and rationales. Introduces Yasmin Khan's video explanation of her conclusions about how voluntary the Indian Army was.	Recall the reasons why soldiers joined the Indian Volunteer Army. Use the video to write a list of the problems that Yasmin Khan identifies. Discuss possible ways of overcoming the problems they identify. Place each source on a spectrum, judging the extent to which it provides evidence to support the idea that the Indian Army was voluntary. Make a tentative judgement in response to the enquiry question, using the evidence that they have considered. Write down their judgement and a brief rationale. List Khan's conclusions and compare them to their own.

▲ Figure C3.2: Example sequence of three lessons for Year 9

Things to notice
1. Students are given the opportunity to reach their own conclusions and to engage independently with source material during these lessons. They also have the thinking of a historian modelled for them through a video. **[C1 & C2]**
2. The connection between historical interpretations and the evidence on which they are based is the driving force of the lesson sequence. The tasks that the students complete mirror this and engage students in thinking about the relationship between sources of evidence and interpretations. **[A4]**

GCSE lessons

Development study example

Development studies explore changes and continuities in a particular theme over time, such as crime and punishment or healthcare. This lesson is taken from the OCR B (SHP) GCSE unit 'The People's Health, 1250–2000'. This unit is taught chronologically, divided into four time periods: medieval, early modern, industrial and modern. Three themes are explored in each period: living conditions, responses to epidemics and efforts to improve public health. This lesson is from the first half of the study and explores similarities and differences between two events that students often confuse.

Enquiry question: Was health in the early modern period just more of the same?	
Builds on a study of medieval public health, and its significant limitations. This included a detailed study of the Black Death in Europe.	Builds towards later study of epidemic disease, when students will compare the responses to cholera, Spanish flu and HIV/AIDS to responses to earlier epidemics.

Purpose of lesson and desired takeaways	Teacher	Students
Lesson question: How were responses to the Great Plague different from the Black Death? **Takeaways:** Changes in response between the medieval and early modern periods: although the plague was the same disease as the Black Death, by the early modern period the public and the government had more sophisticated responses to the disease. Continuities: a lack of advances in understanding the real causes of the disease meant that many ways of responding to plague in the early modern period would have been familiar to medieval people.	Checks student responses to retrieval task and briefly addresses any errors or misconceptions about the Black Death. Guides students through a 1665 Bill of Mortality to draw out, through questioning and modelling, what it reveals about early modern responses: an increase in logical thinking, a more accurate approach to disease and the continuing overwhelming impact of a plague outbreak. Leads a brief discussion comparing the Plague Acts to medieval responses to the Black Death.	Complete retrieval task listing responses of ordinary people and government to the Black Death of 1349. Annotate Bill of Mortality after class discussion with 2-3 key learning points, e.g. 'more rational/scientific thinking.' Read a text about Plague Acts and a summary of other responses to the plague in the early modern period. Complete a graphic organiser which compares the responses to the plague with that of the Black Death. Develop ideas through paired discussion and then feed these into whole-class discussion.

Purpose of lesson and desired takeaways	Teacher	Students
	Teacher circulates to check students' work for accuracy, challenge misconceptions and prompt students to notice more contrasts and similarities, via individual questions or whole-class interventions. Poses key question: why did these responses change? Prompts students to think about changes in the wider context of the period to explain changing responses to the plague.	

▲ Figure C3.3: Example of a development study lesson at GCSE

Things to notice

1. Rather than allowing the sheer amount of substantive content in the GCSE specification to direct the focus of the lesson purely toward the memorisation of substantive content, the lesson is planned around an enquiry question with a disciplinary focus. This directs students' attention both at the substantive and the disciplinary throughout, giving shape and meaning to the substantive content and rendering it more memorable. **[A3]**

2. This lesson does not achieve the intended takeaways as a standalone lesson. As part of an enquiry sequence, it builds on students' prior substantive knowledge of the Black Death from a previous lesson to enable students to think about change and continuity. **[B1]**

3. The lesson is not narrowly focused on a single type of exam question, nor are students coached in following particular routines or formulae for answering questions. Instead, students are engaged in thinking historically so that substantive knowledge and a growing understanding of disciplinary concepts – in this case, change and continuity – is securely encoded. This knowledge, once secure, can be retrieved and deployed in response to several different types of question in an examination. **[D1 & D2]**

Lesson using historical sources

This lesson is taken from a GCSE unit on the British sector of the Western Front during the First World War. The unit is largely examined through questions about sources.

Enquiry question: How can historians find out about the Western Front?		
Builds on chronological overview of the military events of the First World War and knowledge of the physical environments of the Western Front including a trench and a hospital.		Builds towards an understanding of a range of sources historians might use to find out about the Western Front. Students will use this knowledge to answer source utility questions.
Purpose of lesson and desired takeaways	**Teacher**	**Students**
Lesson question: How can historians find out about the Western Front? **Takeaways:** Historians can find evidence in a range of different sources to answer questions about the Western Front. The value of sources is dependent on the historical question being asked.	After checking responses to the recall task and providing feedback, briefly introduces the way historians work. Guides students through types of source that a historian might use to study experiences on the Western Front: diary, oral testimony, military report, etc. Provides students with sets of sources relating to the Western Front (20+ sources) and a list of questions to try to answer. Models selecting evidence which may be useful to answer a particular question. Models critical engagement with one source by evaluating provenance and putting it into context.	Recall task: key features of the Western Front. Note down on mini-whiteboards which sources they think might be particularly useful for finding out about the Western Front. Select sources that they think are useful for answering the questions they have been given. Write short explanations of their reasons for selecting each source and how each source is useful. Do the same thing with three other sources of their choice. Complete a short piece of writing (**not** exam writing) answering the lesson question and drawing upon specific examples of sources that they have used during the lesson.

▲ Figure C3.4: Example of an historic environment lesson at GCSE

Things to notice

1. The approach to assessing students' knowledge and understanding of historical sources at GCSE can lead history teachers to teach students about sources and evidence in a mechanistic way, structured by the rubrics of examination mark schemes. This approach risks obscuring or bypassing the historical knowledge and analytical thinking that underpins a really secure, well-informed answer to such questions. In contrast, this lesson does not directly engage students in answering an examination question, or in the rubrics used to judge an examination answer. Rather, it builds knowledge of historical sources and the analytical process students need to engage in to draw out evidence from sources and evaluate its value for a particular question. Students will subsequently use this knowledge to answer an examination question.

2. This lesson does not achieve the desired takeaways as a standalone lesson. Rather, it plays a role in building up a broader disciplinary understanding of evidence, embedded in substantive knowledge of the Western Front and the sources available to historians to study this particular topic.

Key Stage 5 examples

Specification orientation: both of these examples relate to an A-level thematic study in which students have to explore changes and continuities over a 130-year period. These lessons are part of a thematic exploration of the changing rights of trades union and workers in the USA, 1865–1992.

Lesson building substantive knowledge within a thematic unit

Lesson: American labour and trade union rights in the 1930s

Builds on understanding of the US labour movement between 1865 and 1929. | Builds towards understanding and evaluating interpretations of the New Deal and its impact on workers in the US; understanding the changes in the US labour movement during and after the Second World War.

Purpose of lesson and desired takeaways

Takeaways:	Teacher	Students
The Wagner Act was a key piece of legislation in the story of union rights. Specific terms of the act and reasons why it was a turning point for the unions. Layering up techniques of reading scholarship in ways that helps students 'detect' the interpretation being constructed by the historian.	Sets up a recall task for students to retrieve knowledge relating to this lesson. Uses questioning and class discussion to draw out and assess students' knowledge and thinking. Provides feedback to students by sketching possible shapes of the graph on the board, and questioning students on and discussing with them different possible interpretations and the evidence reasoning to support these. Questions students using mini-whiteboards to test both recall and understanding of the content they have explored for homework.	Retrieve knowledge to sketch a graph of the progress of trade unions and workers between 1865 and 1914. They annotate their graph with reasoning for its shape. Respond using mini-whiteboards. Get out their notes and key events timeline on trade unions and workers 1914–45, for reference during the lesson. Highlight where they notice key arguments or interpretations being expressed in the text. Also highlight any vocabulary that is new to them.

Purpose of lesson and desired takeaways	Teacher	Students
	Gives students a copy of an extract from a piece of historical scholarship about trade unions in this period. This is from a book from which they have already read other extracts in class when studying an earlier period. Reads the text out loud to the class. Pauses regularly to explain new vocabulary in context, as well as to check understanding, via questioning, of the arguments put forward in the text. After students complete judgement task, uses questioning and class discussion to unpack the differing views in the room and the reasoning behind them.	Summarise the arguments being made in the scholarship and make a judgement on a scale saying how far they agree with the historian's view of the Wagner Act.

▲ Figure C3.5: Example of a lesson in a thematic unit at A-level

Things to notice

1. At Key Stage 5, reading historical scholarship with students is likely to be a more organic part of many lessons. Indeed, this forms a critical stepping stone to further academic study, especially in history. The fact that students often study outside of the classroom and come prepared means that reading and discussing historical scholarship can serve to consolidate students' understanding from their independent work, while also adding complexity and nuance to their understanding. **[A4]**
2. Shared reading of scholarship supports the development of substantive and disciplinary knowledge, and an understanding of their interrelationship. It facilitates discussion of the substantive content of the text and of how the historian has arrived at and substantiated their claims.

Lesson exploring interpretations

Lesson question: How and why do historians present such different interpretations of worker's experiences in the Second World War?

Builds on understanding of the US labour movement between 1865 and 1929, as well as experience of handling interpretations in earlier A-level unit and NEA.	Builds towards further exploration of interpretations in the depth studies, which require students to compare two extracts and establish which they find 'more convincing'.

Purpose of lesson and desired takeaways	Teacher	Students
Takeaways: The Second World War was a moment of influence for the unions, as they continued to benefit from the New Deal reforms coupled with the industrial demand of the war. Significantly different interpretations may be offered by different historians, depending on the selection of evidence used. The political viewpoint of a historian may shape the history they write. Zinn is an extreme example, but context influences all historians' interpretations to some extent. Not all interpretations are equally valid. Historians (and students of history) should be critical, and happy to be more or less convinced by different interpretations.	Sets retrieval quiz to check recall of key takeaways from previous lessons. Checks answers and gives feedback. Checks understanding (and completion of) preparatory reading via questioning and summary task. Revisits key ideas about interpretations, using the textbook as an example and showing how opinions and judgements are skilfully presented as certainties. Introduces main comparison task.	Complete short retrieval quiz. Summarise in their own words the interpretation of the Second World War (in the textbook) that they read for homework. Read an extract of historical scholarship from Philip Yale Nicholson, a traditional account of workers during the Second World War. Pick out tone and language which convey interpretation, and summarise the interpretation and evidence offered in support of it. Repeat the task with an extract from Howard Zinn's classic Marxist interpretation. Participate in class discussion.

Purpose of lesson and desired takeaways	Teacher	Students
	Leads discussion about how evidence has been presented by each author, before supporting students to consider which argument they find most convincing.	Write brief notes justifying their choice of 'more convincing' argument.

▲ Figure C3.6: Example of an A-level lesson focusing on interpretations

Things to notice

1. This lesson explores more detail about the Second World War than the students need to remember. This substantive knowledge provides the basis from which students can evaluate different interpretations. The analytical process involved in the evaluation process means that students think hard about the substantive content. As a result, students develop a secure knowledge of the core substantive 'takeaways' required for the course. **[B4]**
2. This lesson, early in the Civil Rights course, introduces students to academic reading and analysis of historical scholarship, distinguishing the subtle nuances of interpretation in the work of different historians. This contributes to students' ongoing learning about the discipline throughout the unit, and indeed the A-level course as a whole. In this way, this lesson contributes to the disciplinary knowledge that students take away with them at the end of the course. **[C4]**

Conclusions

This chapter has briefly summarised the shape some history lessons might take in practice. In each one, whether at Key Stage 3, GCSE or post-16, there is constant attention both to substantive and disciplinary knowledge. Even when working fast to cover specification content, students need structured opportunities to explore the disciplinary in thoughtful ways. It is also worth emphasising that these lessons involve phases of teacher storytelling and exposition, and rich discussions that rely on the teacher's own delivery style and expert knowledge. These outlines give a window into a curriculum being delivered at an individual lesson scale, but inevitably this is like looking at one brick to understand a whole building. Every choice a teacher makes within a lesson is informed by how they are seeking to connect the curriculum as a whole. As always, the teacher is as much the lesson as the plan or the resources.

CHAPTER C4
READING IN THE HISTORY CLASSROOM

Why reading?

Reading is central to history teaching because written prose is at the heart of the work of a historian. Historians communicate historical narrative and analysis in oral or written prose, and textual sources are a significant part of the evidence base for most – although by no means all – historical enquiry. Engaging with written texts is therefore not simply an 'add-on' to support the development of students' literacy, as vital as that is. Written texts have a central curricular role in the development of students' disciplinary knowledge because the text itself, and its status and creation, is often the object of study and because doing history involves the creation of texts (Historical Association, 2021b).

See chapter A3.

History teachers and their students read text in lessons for a wide range of purposes, including (but not limited to):

- to world-build, creating a sense of period or an 'imagined past' (Hill, 2020)
- to tell a story or narrative
- to make an abstract concept more concrete
- to give students access to new vocabulary in context
- to support their understanding of history as a discipline, including how historians draw on evidence and construct and communicate claims (Foster, 2011; Carroll, 2016; Hibbert and Patel, 2019).

David Hibbert and Zaiba Patel used extracts from Yasmin Khan's *The Raj at War* to unpick with students Khan's interpretation and the way in which she drew on source material as evidence to support this. By integrating text in lessons in a range of ways, Tim Jenner argues that it is possible to build a culture of (disciplinary) reading (Jenner, 2019).

See chapter C3.

> Recent Ofsted publications have promoted use of extended texts and reading in the history classroom: see chapter A2.

Narrative and memory

The power of narrative to which cognitive science attests makes narrative – and therefore narrative texts – among the most powerful tools for developing students' substantive knowledge. 'The human mind seems exquisitely tuned to understand and remember stories,' Daniel Willingham explains. He identifies four qualities of narrative that create this memorability: causality, conflict, complications and character (Willingham, 2009). As the Historical Association (2021) points out, 'proper reading adds value to mere information', and when students are immersed in the narrative, argument, mood and tone of a text, it 'builds material in the memory and works on our imagination'. In so doing, it builds worlds (Hill, 2020). History teachers are in an advantageous position to act on this insight and to implement Willingham's recommendation to structure teaching through story, since storytelling lies at the heart of our discipline.

On world-building, see chapter B2.

Narrative and meaning

Narrative texts provide concrete, period-specific encounters with the abstract substantive concepts that students need to grasp to make sense of history. When introducing the concept of colonisation, for example, Mike Hill begins with a short narrative story of a Portuguese settler clearing land on Sao Tomé. By juxtaposing European architecture and livestock, such as sheep, with the sights and sounds of the rainforest, Hill's brief narrative supports students to build a mental picture of a colony, establishing a nascent schema on which students will build through further meaningful encounters (Hill, 2023). This approach to teaching vocabulary in which students infer meaning implicitly from concrete encounters in narrative form is, counter-intuitively, 'much faster and more accurate' than rote learning explicit definitions (Hirsch, 2016).

See the following sections in this chapter and also chapter B4 for further examples of stories used to build worlds.

Using text in the classroom

Reading extended texts in continuous prose in the classroom runs counter to recent trends towards the atomisation of text into bitesize chunks. Alex Quigley (2020) characterises the trend and its risks:

> 'In secondary school, driven by expediency, teachers ... distil complex texts on to the narrow, limited boundaries of the PowerPoint slide. ... Though PowerPoint presentations may offer useable tools for teaching, if they serve as a primary method to reduce the complexity of what our pupils read, then it will inhibit our pupils undertaking the necessary practice of reading extended, complex texts.'

Reversing the trend of reducing the text in a well-intentioned bid to remove barriers for students poses a challenge to history teachers, but one that it is vital, for the reasons outlined – and possible – to overcome. The following sections outline practical ways in which history teachers can do this in the classroom.

Choose your text

A range of types of text may be used in the history classroom, for differing purposes, including:

- narrative texts
- textual primary sources
- extracts from historical scholarship.

The value of narrative texts has been described earlier in this chapter. Meanwhile, engaging students with textual primary sources involves them in the disciplinary process by which historians make inferences from evidence to construct accounts of the past. Sarah Jackson-Buckley and Jessie Phillips (2024), for example, used an extended primary source relating to witchcraft accusations during the European Reformation to engage students in inferences about the web of consequences resulting from the religious upheavals of the period.

To understand the nature and status of historians' accounts of the past, students need to read extracts from historical scholarship, in which historians put forward their interpretations. Students need experience of reading historical scholarship to listen for the 'buzzing' or subtext – to detect how the historian conveys arguments or interpretations – and to analyse and interrogate these (Counsell, 2004).

Many recently published history textbooks, including those designed to support students at GCSE and A-level as well as Key Stage 3, do not fall easily into the categories outlined. Narrative is frequently downplayed, but there is no clear authorial voice or interpretation even in texts designed for A-level students (Fordham, 2017b). This risks misleading students into thinking that there is a single objective 'textbook' version of history, distinct from the more obviously interpretative and argumentative texts of historical scholarship (Paxton, 1999).

Solutions to this include choosing a variety of different texts and textbooks, rather than relying on a single voice. Supplementing A-level textbooks with extended extracts of scholarship, whether articles or chapters, is common at A-level but can be done with younger students too (Jenner, 2019). Prioritising the quality of the narrative when choosing a text can be transformative to the way that students engage with text and its meaning in lessons. Texts aimed at younger readers, such as the *The Silk Roads* (children's edition) and *Black and British: A Short, Essential History* are ideal (Frankopan, 2018; Olusoga, 2020). If the right text is not available, consider writing your own, as increasing numbers of history teachers are doing.

> Chapter B4 includes an example of a story about Marinus van der Lubbe and the Reichstag Fire, written by a teacher as a resource for use in a history lesson. The story is crafted to help students imagine the world of Berlin in 1933, by creating vivid impressions of the street scenes. To show how the fire was a turning point in the rise of the Nazis, the story stays with van der Lubbe in prison as he hears of the destruction of the communists that he had inadvertently caused. The story is closely based on the sources available and does not over-fictionalise details such as dialogue, while immersing students in the world of 1933 Berlin. It attempts to show students what was going on, and the consequences of the events described, rather than telling them about it.

Read your text

Choose techniques to suit your class and to suit different passages of text. A summary of different approaches is given in figure C4.1. The emphasis in all these approaches is on reading text aloud, in most cases with the teacher reading to the class. There are subtle differences between these various approaches, but the central value of reading aloud is the power of prosody for students' comprehension of the meaning of the text. Using emphasis and intonation, pitch and tone, pace and pausing, reading aloud enables us to convey meaning to students, whether the text is a narrative, a primary source text or an interpretation whose 'buzzing' we want students to hear.

See chapter C1 and *WalkThrus* 2 Whole-class reading routines (p. 78).

Teacher reads aloud (*WalkThrus* 2, p. 80)	Read aloud to students without asking them to follow the text, they just listen. Use pace, pitch and tone to bring the story to life. Support with visuals on the screen. Pre-teach some vocabulary if necessary. Read a short section but without interrupting the flow of the narrative.
Teacher storytelling	As above, but tell the story freestyle, based on the text, rather than reading it word for word.
Teacher reads aloud, students follow	Read aloud to students and ask them to follow along in the text. Students may find it helpful to use a ruler to follow the lines. Pause after chunks of text to discuss vocabulary, check for understanding, and engage students in participation, holding them accountable for reading along. Consider pre-teaching some vocabulary to support fluent reading of the text.
Read aloud and paired re-reading (*WalkThrus* 2, p. 81)	Read a section aloud and then ask students to re-read it in pairs prior to completing an activity/questions/notes.
Read aloud and independent read on	Read a section, finish on a cliff-hanger and ask students to read on independently.

Echo reading (*WalkThrus* 2, p. 80)	Choose a particularly dramatic short section of text which lends itself to reading aloud. Read it to students with careful attention to prosody – pace, pitch, tone, emphasis, etc – then ask students to echo read back, copying your model of prosody, individually, chorally or to a partner.
FASE reading (see Lemov, 2021)	A technique to support students in reading aloud fluently. Assign readers rather than asking for volunteers. Ask students to 'start reading' or 'pick up', keeping duration unpredictable and transitions quick, to maximise participation. Pause to discuss, asking students to 'hold your place'. Use teacher reading to bridge between students.
Cloze reading	Read aloud to students, asking them to follow along; pause and signal to students to fill in the next word.

▲ Figure C4.1: Ways to use text in the history classroom

Reading aloud is especially valuable for students' comprehension and acquisition of new vocabulary. As students get older, they encounter new vocabulary largely in written rather than spoken language (Beck, 2013). The emphasis and inflection in spoken language support students in comprehending new vocabulary and the way it is used (Lemov, 2017). Figure C4.2 summarises different ways in which teachers can use text to support vocabulary acquisition. When writing our own texts, we can write them in such a way that the meaning of new vocabulary is explicitly written into the text. When used carefully, pre-teaching vocabulary – particularly for concrete objects with which the students may be unfamiliar – can also support students in accessing texts. It can be quick, active and enjoyable, making use of images, mime and familiar objects in the classroom. This is a finely-balanced curricular decision. Pre-teach too much vocabulary and this can take over curriculum time and become tedious, holding students back from engaging with the fascinating text you have selected; not enough, and they will struggle to access and engage with the text. Abstract concepts are best learned indirectly and inferentially, as discussed earlier in this chapter.

See *WalkThrus* 1 Deliberate vocabulary development (p. 72); *WalkThrus* 2 Pre-reading instructions for complex texts (p. 76).

Pre-teach vocabulary	Pre-teach a few unfamiliar words which are particularly crucial to understanding the story or argument. Be selective – choose the words that are most important. Do it quickly. Use choral repetition for pronunciation. Discuss etymology and word families. Use the words in a sentence – modelled and student-generated. Make it period-specific as far as possible – use this to teach period features and build sense of period.
Use the text to teach vocabulary	Notice where the text teaches/explains vocabulary. This may avoid the need for pre-teaching, but stop and consolidate, using the story, afterwards.
Revise vocabulary	Revisit new vocabulary from a previous lesson when picking up the story in a subsequent lesson.
Use the text to teach concepts	Avoid reducing substantive concepts such as 'parliament' to abstract definitions. Instead, use the text to give concrete meaning and exemplification, then discuss students' developing understanding of the concept afterwards.

▲ Figure C4.2: Ways to use text to support vocabulary acquisition

Engage students in thinking about text

To maximise the impact of reading in the history classroom, students need to engage in thinking about the text, from the meaning of individuals words and phrases to the narrative, the imagined world it conjures, or the 'buzzing' of the author's interpretation. A range of techniques are helpful for this, depending on the text. Jenner (2019) engaged his students in role-play using John Hatcher's account of the Black Death in Walsham in order to make them think deeply about the characters and their reactions as well as the events of the narrative. Christine Counsell (2003) had her students mime carrying a coffin in different ways in order to draw out the interpretation conveyed in the use of a single adverb, 'reverently'. A few approaches that can be used are described in figure C4.2.

See chapters C1 and C3, and *WalkThrus* 3 Role-plays and simulations (p. 158) and *WalkThrus* 2 Summarising academic reading (p. 82).

Principles for reading text in the history classroom

The research and practice discussed can be summarised in the following principles which history teachers observe when using text in the classroom.

1. Make texts routine in your curriculum.
2. Plan enquiries around texts, including texts of historical scholarship.
3. Harness the power of narrative texts.
4. Use extended texts.
5. Read aloud to students.
6. Use historical scholarship (appropriately adapted) from Key Stage 3 (and earlier).
7. Foster a love of reading and culture of scholarship among colleagues and students.

CHAPTER C5
WRITING

In 1945, American Civil War historian William B. Hesseltine wrote that 'writing intellectual history is like trying to nail jelly to the wall'. This problem is of course as much about the jelly as it is the nails or the person with the hammer. History is hard to write. If even the experts find this, it is unsurprising that novice historians face an uphill battle.

There are many factors that make writing in history challenging both to teach and to learn. As a result, writing is, perhaps appropriately, one of the issues most written about in relation to secondary history education.

The challenges of writing in history at school

Hard to learn	Hard to teach
Historical writing can quickly lead to cognitive overload, because students need simultaneously to: • think in a disciplinary way about a particular question, generating their own ideas • structure and organise an answer • retrieve – from memory or notes – and select relevant knowledge • consider syntax, punctuation and grammar, often using recently acquired and context-specific vocabulary • transcribe (the physical act of accurately writing or typing) their ideas. The demands placed on students' cognitive abilities and literacy may be additionally challenging for students with certain types of SEND. Structures of the school day and curriculum allocations for history in secondary schools often leave relatively short chunks of time for students to engage in these complex processes. Historical writing is often tied to assessment, which raises the stakes and means that students are required to complete written tasks independently. Assessed writing is often completed in timed conditions, especially but not exclusively in Years 10–13.	Writing about different disciplinary concepts requires differing approaches. Teaching writing is relatively infrequent because students need enough secure knowledge before attempting extended writing. It is time-consuming, so time devoted to writing practice takes curriculum time away from other aspects. There is a plethora of advice and CPD, both subject-specific and generic, on how to teach writing. It is an area where school leaders often introduce 'cross-curricular' initiatives, which may be distorting to disciplinary writing in history. Writing is hard to assess, making it difficult to diagnose the precise reasons for students' difficulties or the most effective ways to support them. Students transition from Key Stage 2 with limited experience of disciplinary writing in history. Students are taught a variety of approaches to writing in different disciplines and must learn to write differently in different genres and disciplines.

For more on the range of demands placed on students by the act of writing, see:

▲ C5.1: Some difficulties in teaching historical writing

The tension between learning how to write and using writing as the vehicle for assessment presents a particular challenge. See part D for further discussion of written outcomes and assessments.

Figure C5.1 presents a daunting set of challenges. Teachers in all schools are likely to see some effects of these challenges manifest themselves in students' writing. It is worth holding on to what we are trying to achieve.

What does good historical writing look like?

Good historical essay writing by secondary school students, whether aged 11 or 18, answers a historical question with a reasoned argument, emphasising some aspects and downplaying others. The argument is supported by evidence of some kind, whether exemplification or reference to historical source material.

If students can master the art of the paragraph in history, they will be better placed to improve their extended writing. Good paragraphs tend to:

1. make a claim, often in the opening sentence, that expresses a judgement on a single aspect in relation to the question
2. explain the student's thinking behind this claim and the evidence base that substantiates it.

Although students' paragraphs will inevitably (and should) vary in structure, depending on the disciplinary concept being explored or the argument they are trying to articulate, returning repeatedly to these core features will help students acquire metacognitive tools to evaluate and refine their own work.

Importantly, this is not to recommend the 'point, evidence, explain' (PEE) structure or another similarly rigid approach. Although 'PEE' and similar models incorporate the two features identified, they are restrictive. To write history is to 'do' history, constructing an account or interpretation of the past. The writing process is therefore at the heart of students' engagement with the discipline, not an afterthought or bolt-on activity to develop a generic 'literacy'. In the process of writing students must explore and express their own ideas in relation to the question, rather than constructing sentences which fit a prescribed three-part structure or sequence of sentence-openers. Writing is not only more appealing but also less cognitively taxing if students are given a certain degree of flexibility to express their ideas and to write about what they know. This can be achieved by means of a carefully planned learning sequence that builds the requisite substantive and disciplinary knowledge.

> For further discussion of this and other approaches to writing in history, see 'What's the Wisdom on... Extended Writing?' (Historical Association, 2021b).

Avoiding rigid structures and a prescribed sequence of sentences does not preclude the provision of scaffolding in the form of sentence starters, word banks or other forms of support to ease the cognitive overload for students. These kinds of scaffolds can support students' literacy, their retrieval and deployment of historical knowledge, and their disciplinary understanding (Woodcock, 2005).

As they grow confident in constructing paragraphs, students can be taught how these function as units of logical thought within a wider argument.

> Narrative is another genre of historical writing frequently used by historians but differing in its conventions from those of the analytical essay. There are areas of overlap between these genres, including the use of metaphor. The deployment of evidence and interpretation, underpinned by disciplinary concepts such as change or causation, is fundamental to both. Historical narrative still conveys an interpretation, responding to an historical question, although this question may be more implicit. Historical narrative is not 'creative writing' of the kind students may produce in English lessons.
>
> Narrative matters, not because it is a requirement of the current GCSE, but because it is a staple of academic history. Theorisation and exemplification of the teaching of narrative in the secondary history classroom can be found in the following:
>
> - Seán Lang (2003) explored how historians usually write narrative in ways that move far beyond description to sophisticated argument and interpretation.
>
> - Paula Worth (2014) discussed the interplay between scholarship and writing narratives in the classroom.
>
> - Rachel Foster and Kath Goudie (2019) helped students pick apart narratives constructed by historians as a way of modelling how to construct their own.

Teaching all students to write history is tremendously challenging. Few experienced history teachers would claim fully to have succeeded in teaching historical writing, as the plethora of CPD resources, books and articles written on the subject implies. Nevertheless, in an area of practice without easy answers, there are some useful principles to guide history teachers' practice.

Principles for teaching writing in history

1. Keep the history at the heart of writing

Students' writing should answer a well-defined historical question, as discussed in chapter A3 and exemplified in the enquiry questions in chapter B3. These questions all offer a puzzle to solve or a debate with which to engage. The question should bring together the substantive and disciplinary, turning a disciplinary lens on the topic and focusing students' attention on an aspect of disciplinary thinking which is explicitly identified. This creates the opportunity for students to reach and justify well-reasoned historical judgements (Riley, 2000).

Secure, context-specific historical knowledge and vocabulary is a critical prerequisite for students to be able to write historically. This extends beyond factual detail and includes knowledge of disciplinary concepts and the vocabulary to articulate their understanding. Jonathan Sellin (2018) explored the relationship between a student's knowledge, including their disciplinary vocabulary, and their ability to draw meaningful information from source material.

> The Historical Association's 'What's the Wisdom on... Extended Writing?' summarises more fully a selection of research by history teachers into the teaching of historical writing, providing an excellent starting point to explore a range of practical examples.

2. Play the long game

Teaching writing takes a long time. Students need to learn iteratively, testing and honing their skills in response to different questions and deploying different genres and forms of historical writing. Over time, through a range of encounters with reading and writing historical text, students will develop an appreciation of how writing in history is distinct from writing in other disciplines.

In large departments, adopting common language, priorities and frameworks to teach historical writing can help to secure coherent progression for students as they move between different teachers over the years.

3. Embrace writing as an iterative process

In teaching historical writing, process is as valuable as product. Writing is fundamental to learning history; it is not merely a way to display the outcome of learning. Slowly crafting an extended written response gives students time and opportunity to process their understanding and to construct an argument supported by substantive knowledge. Investing time in writing as an iterative process is key to maturing students' historical understanding.

A seminal example of this is James Woodcock's classroom-based research showing how the 'linguistic' can 'release the conceptual' in students' thinking. Woodcock showed how furnishing students with a carefully curated selection of words can simultaneously support their disciplinary thinking and their written explanations of that thinking (Woodcock, 2005). History teachers continue to develop Woodcock's ideas about using language to unlock historical thinking. Sarah Jackson-Buckley and Jessie Phillips (2024) showed how directional language can be used to articulate the complexities of change during the Reformation.

School history writing often diverges from the practice of historians. Much school history writing is assessed. It is frequently high-stakes, completed under time pressure and, in these situations, usually from memory. In contrast, historians draft and re-draft as they research further. Their historical thinking evolves as a result of the process of writing, over a period of time. Students answering GCSE and A-level questions cannot engage in this process within the constraints of an examination.

Nevertheless, allowing students to explore writing as a cycle of planning, drafting, and editing is helpful at every key stage. Not only does this help students to refine the quality of their writing, as Alex Quigley has explored, it also gives them time and space to refine their historical thinking (Quigley, 2022). They will, eventually, become more proficient at planning and writing quickly, for the purposes of assessment; this is one outcome of a slow, steady, incremental process of teaching from Year 7 onwards.

4. Build skill deliberately, not naively

Daisy Christodoulou (2017) distinguishes between naive and deliberate practice, and explains the value of the latter over the former: rather than 'naively' practising the same extended task repeatedly, students benefit from 'deliberately' practising elements of it before putting it all together.

Figure C5.2 details some ways we might do this when teaching historical writing.

Instead of 'naively...'	...deliberately...
...repeatedly writing whole essays,	• create plans that organise ideas into paragraphs. • decide which knowledge is relevant to a question. • discuss how multiple paragraphs combine into an argument, emphasising some aspects and downplaying others. • read the work of historians and see how they present ideas. • discuss vocabulary, imagery or metaphor that might be helpful to articulate the disciplinary aspect of a specific question (Carroll, 2024). • write single paragraphs, or even sentences, and give feedback on them.
...repeatedly practising exam questions,	• model and practise identifying the substantive and disciplinary focus of a specific question. • list key words you would expect to see in an answer. • provide a detailed pre-made plan to free up students' cognitive capacity to practice writing.

▲ Figure C5.2: Examples of 'naive' vs. 'deliberate' practice in writing

This deliberate practice is often overlooked as a key part of learning disciplinary writing or is assumed to be in place already, but working at word, sentence and paragraph level brings huge gains whether in Key Stage 3, at GCSE or post-16..

Working at a sentence level, for example, is helpful throughout the process of learning to write. It is not a question of 'sentences in Year 7, paragraphs in Year 8, essays in Year 9' or similar simplistic models of progression. Indeed, students in upper Key Stage 2 regularly write in paragraphs. Rather, we need to teach students how to construct these elements using new substantive and disciplinary knowledge, and how they work in different genres of historical writing, for example as components of a wider argument.

Finally, when teaching writing, it is tempting to use lots of supporting resources – mnemonics, writing frames, sentence starters and so on – to ease the cognitive load for students. Any scaffolding must be removed over time, however, while maintaining the quality achieved when using the scaffold. This is hard to do (Evans and Pate, 2007).

The 'deliberate practice' approach builds writing skills differently, with less scaffolding to fade away from students as they gain expertise (Richards, 2021). For example, a teacher might introduce a type of writing by drafting a paragraph in that style, writing it a sentence at a time and explaining what role each sentence and even particular phrases are playing. This slowing down of the process to look carefully at the thinking behind it effectively builds a student's metacognitive understanding of different elements of writing in history.

> James Carroll is a leading researcher of writing in the secondary history classroom, particularly with A-level students. His work is rooted in concrete examples of classroom practice.
>
> - In his blog 'Duplo to watercolours', Carroll (2018b) explores the benefits of blurring the distinction between the substantive and disciplinary in students' writing, rather than trying to separate these strands.
>
> - In 'Terms and conditions: using metaphor to highlight causal processes' (2022), he explores how metaphors can add genuine precision to how students express their disciplinary thinking.
>
> - For those interested in oracy in a history a classroom and how this might convert to improvements in the quality of students' writing, read Carroll's 2017 article about oral rehearsal of arguments.

5. Build on what students already know:

From Year 7 history teachers can develop the broad writing knowledge gained at primary level into discipline-specific forms. Ways to do this include:

- Be clear about what historical writing is (narrative, causal explanation, analysis of evidence or interpretation) and is not (creative writing, chronological recounting from a supposed neutral perspective).
- Explicitly distinguish historical writing from writing in other disciplines (see the following section).
- Build on grammatical knowledge taught at Key Stage 2: for example, show how modal verbs, to which every Year 6 student has been introduced, can be used by historians to express uncertainty, for example when drawing tentative conclusions based on limited or incomplete evidence from sources. Spotlight other aspects of grammar, such as how Foster (2013) uses geographical metaphors to explain change, which can help historians unlock masses of pre-existing knowledge.

6. Beware of cross-curricular stumbling blocks

Students understandably find acclimatising to writing in different disciplines challenging. This is exacerbated by generic solutions used by teachers or mandated by senior leaders. One common example is 'point, evidence, explain' or 'PEE' paragraphing, which teachers 'adapt' to their own subject.

Problems can quickly emerge if such prescriptive frameworks are adopted school-wide. What constitutes 'evidence' or 'explanation' is very different in geography, in history and in English. Talking to colleagues in other departments can help history teachers to identify likely misconceptions and plan to address these in their teaching of historical writing.

Conclusions

This section does not provide a comprehensive guide to teaching writing in the secondary history classroom. Rather, it is intended as a useful starting point to reflect on how we approach this vital but challenging aspect of the discipline. These principles are designed to help teachers plan effective teaching of historical writing, but as ever, careful consideration must be given to how they can be enacted in specific contexts. For example, writing about sensitive and controversial historical events would require additional considerations. Likewise, writing is often seen as a viable 'whole school area for development'. Working with generic 'whole school' expectations can militate against disciplinary approaches; the principles outlined in this chapter may help to mitigate this.

Finally, in a crowded curriculum, writing is often used for a dual purpose, as an assessed outcome as well as a learning process. This can reduce the scope for explicit teaching, deliberate practice and timely formative feedback, making it even harder for students to hone the craft of historical writing and to get at least some of Hesseltine's 'jelly' to stick to the wall. Chapters D1 and D2 will further explore approaches to assessment and outcomes, and the balance between teaching and assessment.

Part D

CHAPTER D1
OUTCOMES

History teachers must find ways for students to communicate their understanding of the past. Planned, explicit expressions of students' understanding will occur in most lessons. For example, students might discuss initial reflections on an enquiry question, recall prior knowledge to make sense of current learning, begin to categorise their substantive knowledge into causal factors and later discuss prioritisation or links between causal factors, or begin to weigh historical arguments.

See chapter A2 for a summary of developments in history teaching including consideration of what constitutes rigorous history teaching.

The creation of authentic historical outcomes, answering genuinely historical questions, communicating understanding of the past through the lens of history, is vital to students' learning. This chapter explores what history teachers should look for in terms of student outcomes and how they can judge the quality of these.

Enquiry questions to shape outcomes

Enquiry questions are used in history education to 'govern learning across a short sequence of lessons' (Riley, 2000); they provide cohesion and a sense of direction. They should be shared explicitly with students, ideally throughout the sequence of lessons (Dawson, n.d.). The enquiry question structures the historical process for students, supporting them to construct, build and revise their response with some degree of independence.

See chapter A1 for ways in which school history emulates the practice of historians. See chapter A3 for enquiry questions, and chapter A2 for developments in approaches to using enquiry questions.

Each historical enquiry should allow students to develop their substantive knowledge (people, events and developments, chronology and period-specific features, and historical terms), and their understanding of history as a discipline. The production of an outcome requires students to organise and synthesise historical knowledge before communicating it.

See chapter A3 for disciplinary and substantive knowledge.

Appropriate outcome tasks

Genuinely historical outcome tasks will allow students to draw together learning from an enquiry and to develop their ideas and historical thinking. An outcome task is not necessarily synonymous with assessment, however. While an outcome task in history should give students the opportunity to synthesise and communicate substantive and disciplinary knowledge, the purpose of assessment is to shed light on the impact of our curriculum: to determine whether students have learned what we intended them to learn. An outcome task may also be used for assessment purposes, but this is not its sole or primary function in students' learning.

See chapter D2.

The curricular function of outcome tasks in students' learning is one reason why use of GCSE-style questions as outcome tasks at Key Stage 3 is inappropriate. GCSE questions are used for summative assessment. They are designed for reliable and consistent assessment of successive national cohorts of students. For this reason they are mechanistic and reductive of the discipline. Moreover, each question typically tests a very small sample of the domain. GCSE examination questions are not designed for – and thus are poorly suited to – creating opportunities for students to synthesise substantive and disciplinary knowledge in response to an enquiry question studied over several lessons. At Key Stage 3, history teachers have freedom to shine a light on the past from a wide range of disciplinary angles and to teach students to engage with disciplinary concepts in a variety of ways, guided by the topic and the scholarship. For consistency, GCSE questions approach disciplinary concepts such as causation more narrowly, always requiring similar kinds of analytical approaches, determined by the substantive content of the particular unit. These approaches are not suitable for transplant on to enquiries about completely different topics and periods at Key Stage 3, even where the disciplinary focus, causation for example, may be similar.

> Recent Ofsted publications provide guidance on how history teachers can prompt students to communicate historical thinking, including a specific caution not to use GCSE-style questions to frame assessment at Key Stage 3: see chapter A2.

When designing outcome tasks – as when planning the enquiry as a whole – history teachers need to think about the substantive content and the disciplinary lens through which this is being taught, as well as the interplay between these. Turning to the conventions of history as a discipline and its forms of accounting will guide history teachers in planning outcome tasks. The following questions may be useful guides to planning:

- Has the immediate sequence of lessons explicitly prepared students for creating the outcome?
- Is the outcome a logical way for students to wrestle with the enquiry question?
- Does the outcome allow students to communicate relevant disciplinary knowledge?
  - Example: curating a guidebook for a museum display may allow students to develop and communicate ideas about historical significance.
- Do students have the substantive knowledge needed to complete a particular outcome well?
  - Example: if writing a piece of historical fiction, do students have a sufficient depth of hinterland knowledge and sense of period to make informed authorial choices?

Strong enquiry questions knit together the substantive and disciplinary and, in many cases, an appropriate outcome task may be for students simply to answer the enquiry question. This will require students to synthesise substantive and disciplinary knowledge. Extended written outcomes, such as an essay, are frequently used to allow students to draw together their knowledge and thinking. The construction of narrative can also convey depth of knowledge and complex historical thinking to the same end. As Lang (2003) and others have shown, narrative need not be regarded as simplistic or of lesser value than an analytical essay. In either case, outcome tasks practising extended disciplinary writing allow students to develop familiarity with and the ability to observe the conventions of the discipline, building their historical literacy.

See chapters A2 and A3 for discussion of enquiry questions.

In-period and out-of-period historical writing

Historical writing can take two forms. In-period writing involves students using deep knowledge of a period to explore a theme, society or event from a contemporary perspective, whether writing in the first person or third person. Examples include a newspaper report, letter written as if by someone at the time, or historical fiction. This is the mode of writing of historical novelists. Out-of-period writing, the mode of academic and popular history, involves students communicating historical analysis, in the third person, from their present perspective. This might be in the form of an analytical essay or narrative, a podcast or documentary script, or museum display.

It is easy to underestimate the challenges of in-period writing, particularly the depth of period knowledge required. Moreover, when engaged in in-period writing, students by definition cannot adopt the historian's perspective and so history teachers must think carefully about when this mode is suited to the historical thinking that they want students to do. Teachers will need to provide careful modelling and scaffolding with clear criteria to support students in maintaining a tight focus and deploying their knowledge effectively. For in-period writing to be historically accurate, it requires a depth and breadth of period knowledge. This applies to the topic (for example, the character or themes explored in the case of historical fiction) but also the language used, which must show sensitivity to the period. Another way to avoid anachronisms is to ensure in-period writing is plausible, including asking students to write in a genre that is not anachronistic to the time period.

> The Historical Association's 'Write Your Own Historical Fiction Competition' includes a teachers' guide to using and writing historical fiction in the classroom, including recorded webinars with author Tony Bradman:
>
>
>
> The Historical Association's Young Quills award reviews and awards prizes to the best historical fiction for young people each year and shortlisted texts are an ideal resource for use in the classroom or to supplement the curriculum.

History teachers have devised a range of alternative authentic outcomes other than the traditional essay or narrative which still allow students to communicate their historical knowledge and thinking (figure D1.1). Where the outcome is closely matched to the enquiry, these can be particularly powerful for inviting students to engage in the methodological choices involved in historians' work, such as the selection and use of source material, and the process of establishing links and relationships to build historical arguments. Particular types of task can serve to emphasise the different disciplinary methods and lenses through which historians study the past and communicate interpretations. For these reasons, outcome activities such as these are both valuable outcomes in their own right and can be helpful precursors to extended writing.

Museum displays	Use of artefacts
Curating a museum display can be a suitable outcome for enquiries exploring significance, interpretations and/or evidence.	Gabriella West and Sarah Longair made an object (a silver casket from Mysore) the vehicle through which students learned about British colonisation of India (West and Longair, 2023). The outcome of a sequence of lessons was for students to compose a narrative of the life cycle of the silver casket which situated the artefact within a wider history of the Mughal and British Empires in India in order to draw conclusions about these empires and the relationship between them.
For example, students might select several artefacts, images, maps or documents to tell a particular story (or stories) about the life of Eleanor of Aquitaine. Explanation and justification of the rationale for their selection, for example how certain artefacts or sources illuminate certain themes, would allow students to demonstrate their understanding of evidence, interpretations and historical significance. A leaflet or advert explaining students' curatorial choices is key to maintaining a disciplinary focus in this kind of task, preventing the focus slipping to layout and artistic presentation, and ensuring students' thinking is made explicit.	

Creating a diagram	Annotating/evaluating a historical reconstruction drawing
Diagrams are useful ways to help students to articulate their understanding. For example, they could create two diagrams of a village, the first showing it before 1066 and the second in 1086 to show post-Conquest changes and continuities. Alternatively, a change diagram could take the form of 'theme circles' – a circle of each different area of change in a given period of time, filled with specific examples of 'before and after' pairings. The size of each circle could reflect the scale of that area of change. A diagram analysing causation could show different causes linked to one another and to an outcome, in the form of a web. Students might annotate each cause with evidence, and each connecting line with their reasoning regarding the causal connection. See for example Counsell et al., 2024, chapter 12.	Using historical reconstruction artwork as interpretations fosters discussion of the choices and compromises needed to construct a version of the past. For example, students could annotate an interpretation by Alan Sorrell or Ivan Lapper, detailing the way the artist has chosen to present a historical moment or how they used the available evidence to inform their art. 'Look and Learn' has an online database of artistic interpretations: www.lookandlearn.com.

▲ Figure D1.1: Examples of authentic outcome tasks other than essays

Tailoring outcome tasks to enquiry questions

The examples in figure D1.1 represent several forms of genuine historical outcomes, but these cannot be deployed indiscriminately at the end of any enquiry. Particular types of outcome task are more appropriate for particular types of enquiry question. For example, writing a narrative is often particularly suited to allowing students to communicate their understanding of change/continuity, or of causation over a short period of time. James Ellis (2020) researched how blending micro-narratives of individuals in Stalin's Russia with a macro-narrative allowed his students to produce historical narratives in response to the question, 'How did Stalin change the lives of the Russian people?'. In creating historical narratives, Ellis found his students used 'topic knowledge to introduce a section of their narrative, used specific detailed knowledge to support this or to add depth, and then used a micro-narrative to add depth and further illustrate their point'. In this way, students were able to characterise change in Stalin's Russia. Ellis prepared his students carefully through his planning and teaching of the whole enquiry sequence, considering how blending macro- and micro-narratives over the course of the enquiry would provide students with the knowledge they needed and support them in the thinking required to create their narratives.

Outcome tasks to avoid

The key to assessing the rigour and suitability of an outcome task is to consider whether it allows students to communicate their historical knowledge and thinking with as much complexity and sophistication as possible. The following types of outcome tasks are likely to be less valuable and therefore not a worthwhile investment of students' time (or conducive to use for assessment purposes).

Model-making

While cardboard motte-and-bailey castles are a staple in some history departments, they are not well-suited to supporting secondary-age students to communicate their understanding in response to a rigorous enquiry question. For example, they do not allow students to consider the purpose, role or significance of castles. Any of these ideas can be more easily captured through other tasks, such as creating a guidebook to tell the story over time of a specific castle. Building cardboard castles places the analytical focus on engineering cardboard structures while (to cite Daniel Willingham (2009) talking about his daughter's experience of history education) making cookies for a project on the Underground Railroad leads students to think about cookies, not history. In either case, the emphasis is not on historical thinking.

Diaries, drama and role play

Where available, diaries are invaluable as source material in history lessons but setting the creation of diary entries for real or fictional historical characters as an outcome activity is less so. The attempt to foster empathy and to demonstrate understanding of sense of period through the writing of a first-hand account often leads to poor in-period historical writing. It can be highly insensitive, for example, when

See chapter C2

such tasks are set in relation to emotive and controversial topics such as slavery or the Holocaust. Attempts to replicate or mirror the sensitivities, concerns or motives of people from the past downplay and risk diminishing the actual experiences of individuals, groups and societies. Similar caveats apply to student-devised role play or drama.

Posters

These might make for a colourful classroom display, but they rarely allow students to develop or communicate their historical thinking with the same degree of sophistication or complexity as other outcomes. As an outcome task, posters typically serve to summarise factual material relating to a topic. Students' attention is usually devoted to thinking about non-historical aspects, such as presentation and bubble-writing. A poster might, however, be used with greater sophistication to present a diagram such as those suggested in figure D1.1.

Social media

The use of different types of social media to present or frame historical arguments and claims, or to synthesise a large amount of material, is also ahistorical because it is anachronistic. It is not a genre well suited, as users of social medial are aware, to the presentation of nuanced and well-supported historical analysis.

For teacher-devised and directed drama, role play and simulation, see chapter C2.

These links will take you to a varied range of outcome tasks, compiled by Andrew Wrenn, which have been tried and tested by history teachers:

CHAPTER D2
WAYS TO ASSESS FOR DIFFERENT PURPOSES

The previous chapter discussed the outcomes we might ask students to produce in history. The creation of authentic, historical outcomes, answering genuinely historical questions and communicating understanding of the past, is vital to students' learning. It is also our responsibility, as teachers, to assess the impact of our curriculum: to find out whether students have learned the things we intended them to learn. Assessment, therefore, is essential.

> See chapter A2 for developments in approaches to assessment.

Purposes of assessment

At its simplest, the purpose of assessment is to find out whether students have learned what we intended them to learn. This is commonly and helpfully subdivided into formative and summative purposes. Formative assessment is finding out what students know and can do in order to inform our teaching and improve students' learning. Summative assessment is finding out what students know and can do to inform a judgement about them at a particular point in time, for example at the end of a unit, term, course or key stage.

Different types of assessment are suited to these different purposes. To reach a summative judgement about what students have learned by a given point, the assessment should sample widely from the curriculum taught. A test on only the most recent topic will not give us a good basis for a summative judgement about a student's knowledge of the curriculum as a whole (Christodoulou, 2016, pp. 59–60).

Formative assessment, by contrast, is most useful when it is precisely focused on a particular area of knowledge. A carefully targeted quiz, timeline or short question can support more precise inferences about what students do or do not know, and so inform our teaching (Carr and Counsell, 2014). We might realise that we need to reteach the chronology of the escalating conflict between Charles I and parliament in the 1640s or address a particular misconception with regard to a substantive concept, such as colonisation, or an aspect of disciplinary knowledge, such as change/continuity or interpretations.

Figure D2.1 summarises some differences between formative and summative assessment which point towards the need for different methods to realise these differing objectives.

Formative assessment	Summative assessment
Enables learning (assessment for learning)	Assesses the results of learning (assessment of learning)
Frequent, embedded in teaching	Infrequent
Assesses what knowledge (substantive and/or disciplinary) students have 'at their fingertips' in the moment	Assesses a 'residue' of substantive and knowledge
Samples a small area of the domain, precisely targeted to allow specific inferences to be made about students' knowledge or understanding	Samples broadly from the domain of knowledge, using a range of different question types or assessment methods
Quick to administer and assess, providing rapid and specific feedback to teacher and student	Takes sufficient time to implement the outlined effectively, balancing this against costs in curriculum time for teaching and formative assessment
Diagnostic – to establish immediate micro-curricular actions or adjustments needed to improve the student's knowledge and understanding (not necessarily the work)	Holistic – to support judgements about student attainment and inferences about progress
Informs small-scale, short-term actions by students and teachers.	Informs large-scale evaluation of curriculum and pedagogy, and the ongoing process of curriculum and teacher development by teachers and leaders.

▲ Figure D2.1: Comparing summative and formative assessment (with thanks to the Historical Association)

Using essay questions for assessment purposes

> Ms Shaw plans an essay as the outcome of the current enquiry for her class. She plans a series of activities that will prepare students for the analytical, disciplinary thinking involved as well as the substantive knowledge they will need. These might include card sorts, planning diagrams and oral rehearsal. Ms Shaw provides a model paragraph or structure, or show-calls a student's work under the visualiser as a model, providing feedback to students and encouraging self-assessment during the process. She circulates the room and reads students' work, providing live feedback or prompts to students, and answering their questions. All of these are methods of teaching and support students' learning. With practice, students will require less support and/or be able to tackle more complex essay questions involving the synthesis of more abstract or otherwise challenging content.
>
> At the end of the essay-writing lesson, moreover, Ms Shaw has a wealth of knowledge about her students' knowledge and understanding, even before she reads the students' work. She knows not only what kind of support the students needed but also how much, as well as being able to see in students' written work how they responded to prompts and what they did with what they knew. This knowledge will inform her feedback to students and the planning of subsequent lessons, including the teaching approaches she uses to prepare the class for their next essay.

Extended written outcomes such as the typical essay are frequently used for formative assessment in history classrooms, with formative feedback provided to students. They are, however, difficult for teachers to use formatively, and the feedback provided to students can be difficult for them to use. Extended analytical writing in history is a complex process, requiring students to synthesise information and structure argument. It tests not only their knowledge and understanding of substantive content and disciplinary concepts but also their ability to organise and structure their ideas and to communicate these in writing. Writing an historical narrative is similarly synoptic and poses similar, if not identical, challenges.

When students perform well on an extended written task, this is a good indication of their security in each of these areas of the domain. When students perform poorly, however, it can be difficult for the teacher to diagnose the reason or reasons. Was it a lack of substantive knowledge, a weakness in disciplinary understanding, a failure to plan a clear structure, or a working memory overwhelmed by the challenge of forming letters on the page at the root of the student's difficulties?

It is likely, of course, that a combination of these is responsible, but the essay alone does not allow precise inferences to be drawn to inform teaching. A range of smaller, more limited assessment tasks is therefore helpful for formative assessment, allowing more precise diagnosis of students' knowledge and understanding in different areas. These can be used to inform teaching before students subsequently tackle the essay. A number of examples are included in Figure D2.2.

Essays still have a vital role in formative assessment in history, however. The feedback loop is not the only process shaping or enabling learning in formative assessment tasks. The process of writing an essay is a learning process for students. It inducts them into history's methods of accounting, consolidates their knowledge and develops their analytical, disciplinary thinking. Students learn from the experience, as in the example outlined in the box. It is, nevertheless, difficult to use as a formative assessment tool.

See chapters C5, D1 and D4.

For these reasons, a strong case has been made by Fordham, Counsell and others for the separation or decoupling of formative and summative assessment (Fordham, 2017c; Counsell, 2023). Different methods of assessment are appropriate for different purposes, as the following sections outline. Endeavouring to use the same task for both summative and formative purposes can create difficulties for teachers or require compromises that render the assessment less than suitable for either purpose.

Formative assessment

> At the start of a lesson, Mr Khan asks his class to write a timeline of five key events in the reign of Charles I, drawing on students' knowledge from two or three previous lessons addressing the enquiry question, 'When did the Puritans come closest to a revolution in England?' Students write these on mini-whiteboards, so that he can quickly gauge the knowledge of the whole class.
>
> Mr Khan knows that the events of 1629 are crucial to students' understanding the significance of Parliament's recall in 1640 and the shift in the balance of power between Charles and the Puritans that results. He notices that students recalled at least one out of Charles's marriage to Henrietta Maria and his persecution of Puritans in the 1630s, but that some students omitted the dissolution of Parliament in 1629.
>
> Mr Khan reminds students of the dissolution of Parliament in 1629 and adjusts his teaching during this lesson and the next, including the way that he teaches the events of 1640, in light of this. By the end of the lesson, or the following lesson, students' knowledge of the key events of Charles's reign has changed. Mr Khan checks this, targeting some individuals identified during the lesson. The assessment has served its purpose but the 'data' it provided is now out of date.

This example illustrates the characteristics of formative assessment set out in figure D2.1.

To realise their curricular aims, history teachers seek to instil a range of different kinds of knowledge in their students. History's semantic gravity means that while historians necessarily make generalisations, without which it is not possible to say anything at all, those generalisations are firmly anchored in the particular. Consequently, detailed knowledge, in the form of individual stories and experiences, is vital both to history and history teaching. Most of this precise detail is the hinterland of knowledge which sits around the core – the generalisations – which is the residue of knowledge we want students to be left with. The residue is the takeaways students will know when they finish the curriculum. It is impossible, however, for students to learn the core knowledge, and to retain this as 'residue', without traversing the hinterland (Dawson, 2008; McCrory, 2015; Grande, 2022).

See chapter B4.

This has implications for assessment, as Grande has explored (Grande, 2022; 2023). It means that the hinterland knowledge we teach students – often the main focus of large parts of each lesson – is vital at the time, and during the particular enquiry, but its importance fades over time. History teachers teach a great deal of knowledge which they expect and intend students to forget over time, but which will leave a core residue of long-term knowledge (Counsell, 2017; 2000; Grande, 2023).

Within an enquiry, the precise, detailed knowledge of the hinterland must be secure, however. In the short term, while teaching the enquiry, teachers therefore need to assess whether this hinterland knowledge is secure and readily recalled – at students' fingertips. Moreover, in a well-sequenced curriculum, some of the finer details, the hinterland, of one enquiry may be useful fingertip knowledge in a subsequent enquiry a short time later. We may therefore want to assess some of these finer details and use retrieval practice to strengthen their retention, in the short or medium term, to support subsequent learning (Counsell, 2017).

See chapters A3 and B4.

A range of different diagnostic assessment tools are therefore useful to assess students' security in different kinds of knowledge and at different stages of the curriculum journey. While each individual method of assessment used should be limited in scope and precisely targeted to inform specific feedback and actions by teachers and students, a wide range of different methods are appropriate to assess different types of knowledge. Figure D2.2 sets out several methods suitable for formative assessment in history and the circumstances in which these may be useful.

Timing	Method of assessment	Rationale
Within a lesson or enquiry, to assess fingertip knowledge required in the short term	Timeline	To check for secure knowledge of the sequence of events relevant to a particular enquiry
	Quizzing, including multiple-choice or short-answer questions; oral or written; mini-whiteboards or other whole-class response methods might be used	To check for secure knowledge of key people, events, places and changes
	Questioning; choral responses, mini-whiteboards or cold-calling might be used for sampling responses	To check for security in key aspects of knowledge relating to the current lesson/enquiry, including to check for listening and comprehension
	Questions prompted by a stimulus such as an image or map	Stimulus provides a trigger to retrieval of knowledge
	Concluding sentences or paragraphs of argument, oral or written	Check and provide feedback on students' developing ability to answer the enquiry question; written answers may prepare for or follow on from oral debate (or both)
	Enquiry outcome task	Assesses how well students can synthesise substantive and disciplinary knowledge to answer the enquiry question

Timing	Method of assessment	Rationale
Between enquiries, for formative assessment of residue knowledge students need to retain in the long term	Timelines, including comparative timelines	To check for secure chronological sequencing of periods/topics, including concurrent or overlapping periods and events in different geographical locations
	Quizzes including multiple-choice questions	To test for residue knowledge of key takeaways, e.g. substantive concepts or security in key features of a period, to check for misconceptions
	Short answers (paragraphs) about a substantive concept or disciplinary knowledge, e.g. how historians use sources	Assesses knowledge of these concepts and what knowledge students can draw on to illustrate these; informs subsequent teaching of these in the classroom

▲ Figure D2.2: Methods of formative assessment in history

Summative assessment

From time to time, a history teacher will want to assess whether the intended residue of knowledge – the curricular takeaways – has been retained. Summative assessment needs to assess whether students know and can do the things we want them to remember and be able to do in the long-term. This is what will provide the foundations or frameworks that enable students to make sense of new knowledge, expanding their schemata over time.

Individually, the methods outlined in figure D2.2 are unsuited to summative assessment. Each samples too narrowly from the curriculum to support a summative judgement about a student's knowledge of the curriculum as a whole. An aggregation of the approaches suggested for use between enquiries, sampling knowledge across the curriculum, can be ideal for summative purposes, however. Tasks such as timelines and multiple-choice questions are relatively quick to complete, so that a number of such questions can be set, which makes it easier to sample knowledge from a wide range of topics. This sample serves as a proxy measure of students' knowledge of the curriculum as a whole (Fordham, 2017d, p. 288).

Teachers need to be careful, however, to ensure that a summative assessment is indeed a good proxy for, or sample of, the knowledge they intended students to retain: the intended core, residue knowledge. At Key Stage 3, Grande, following Counsell, suggests that these curricular takeaways may be broad, general and abstract, rather than detailed and precise. Questions targeting fine-grained detail that was essential fingertip knowledge during a particular enquiry, but which students do not need to retain, may not be a good proxy measure of whether students have retained the residue of core knowledge. Students may score poorly, having forgotten – as they were expected to – these precise details; as Grande suggests, however, this may not be a concern (Grande, 2023).

A different question might uncover that students have, in fact, retained the residue of knowledge intended as an outcome of the curriculum. Grande has developed ways to assess residue knowledge of his curriculum takeaways through the use of multiple-choice questions deploying 'unknown particulars' (figure D2.3). These test students' security in concepts and generalisations, such as early 20th-century militarism, by assessing their ability to apply their knowledge to an unfamiliar but related example (Grande, 2023; 2024b).

Question	Answers	Notes
Bretenaldo was a French man who went on a pilgrimage around the year 1000. What was most likely to have been the reason for his pilgrimage?	A: to trade goods B: to spread knowledge C: to visit holy relics D: to fight for his king	Tests residual understanding of the concept of pilgrimage. Students have not studied Bretenaldo but have studied examples of pilgrimage. This question tests whether the curriculum has left a residue or takeaway knowledge of the cult of the saints and pilgrimage in medieval Christian Europe.

Question	Answers	Notes
Helmuth von Moltke, the chief of the German Army in 1914, was a militarist leader. What was von Moltke most likely to think?	A: Germany should create an army. B: Everyone in Germany should join the German army. C: Germany should make an alliance with the country with the strongest army. D: Germany should use war to prevent Russia gaining military superiority. E: Germany should declare war on Britain to prevent Britain gaining naval superiority.	Tests understanding of the concept of militarism. Students have not encountered von Moltke in the curriculum. This question tests whether the examples of militarism that they have studied have left a sufficiently secure residual understanding of the concept for them to be able to reason their way to the answer.
Sir Thomas Roe spent four years in Emperor Jahangir's royal court. Where would Sir Thomas Roe have spent his time while at the royal court?	A: Roe would have stayed near Jahangir's capital, Agra. B: Roe would have travelled around the Ottoman Empire. C: Roe would have followed Jahangir around the Mughal Empire. D: Roe would have spent time in the place where people were put on trial.	Tests understanding of the concept of the royal court in the Mughal Empire, and checks for common misconceptions. Students have not studied Roe, but have encountered the royal court in their study of the Mughal Empire.

▲ Figure D2.3: Multiple-choice questions devised by Jonathan Grande and his team at Ark Schools to assess residue knowledge through 'unknown particulars'

Assessment of the curriculum at Key Stage 3 may differ in this way from summative assessment at Key Stages 4 and 5, where examinations do require students to have very detailed

See chapters B2, B3 and C3.

knowledge at their fingertips to answer the questions which sample from the specification. The purposes and intended outcomes of a history curriculum at Key Stage 3, however, are generally concerned with establishing the underlying foundations or frameworks of knowledge, both substantive and disciplinary, which will allow students to succeed in their study of a relatively narrow selection of themes, periods and topics at Key Stages 4 and 5.

Essay questions in summative assessment

An essay question, difficult to use for formative purposes, as discussed already, is well suited to summative purposes, since it requires students to synthesise their knowledge, and the range of responses allows for distinctions to be drawn between the degree of success of different students, which may be required for ranking or grading students' outcomes relative to one another.

An essay question, nonetheless, still tends to assess students' knowledge of one particular topic. Synoptic questions which ask students to draw on their knowledge of a number of different topics can also be used in order to draw on a wider sample of students' knowledge, giving a better proxy for their knowledge of the curriculum as a whole (Carr, 2024). Synoptic summative assessment is also helpful for ironing out variation in students' performance between different assessments, which can be difficult for students, parents and non-specialist leaders to interpret.

> **Examples of synoptic questions which might be used for summative assessment in Key Stage 3 history**
>
> How were different places you have studied in history connected?
>
> Who had power in the medieval world?
>
> How did revolutions transform the world between [date] and [date]?
>
> What have you learned about empires [or another substantive concept] during the periods of history you have studied this year?
>
> What kinds of evidence can historians use to study the medieval world [or other topic(s)]?
>
> Why do historians arrive at different interpretations of history? Refer to some of the topics you have studied in your answer.

Figure D2.4 outlines some approaches to summative assessment and how they can be used.

Method of assessment	Rationale
Timeline	Assess security of chronological framework across the curriculum (so far).
Multiple-choice questions targeting residue substantive or disciplinary knowledge, for example using 'unknown particulars' (see Grande 2024a).	Assess security of knowledge of substantive and disciplinary curriculum takeaways.
Concept question	Assesses knowledge of a substantive or disciplinary concept and students' ability to illustrate this with concrete examples and to draw points of comparison between different places and time periods.
Reading passage (unseen passage from historical scholarship)	Tests students' ability to deploy different types of knowledge acquired during the year to make sense of an historian's argument.
Overarching (synoptic) essay question	Assesses students' ability to deploy knowledge from across several topics in the curriculum and to synthesise this to answer a historical question with a focus on a disciplinary concept (for example, change, causation, evidence or interpretations), making and supporting generalisations.

▲ Figure D2.4: Methods of summative assessment in history

CHAPTER D3
MARKING, GRADING AND MAKING JUDGEMENTS

Is it necessary or useful to mark students' work in history? In practice, the answer depends on what is meant by 'marking', and the purpose of the assessment. As discussed in chapter D2, assessments may fulfil a number of different purposes. Marking is generally associated with individual (hand)written feedback on students' work. There are other approaches that teachers can take to students' work, both for formative and summative purposes. Traditional personalised written marking is time-consuming for teachers to do, with implications for workload. The value to students' learning in history may not be sufficiently great to justify the time spent.

> See chapter D2. See also chapter A2 for developments in approaches to assessment in history teaching.

Formative assessments

The purpose of formative assessment is diagnostic: to inform small-scale, short-term actions by students and teachers in order to improve the students' knowledge and understanding.

Much formative assessment in history lessons is ephemeral. It is carried out in the classroom, through questioning and quizzing, and through the range of different activities history teachers use to get their students thinking, from mind-maps to card sorts, role plays to choral response. Teachers may check the answers of a whole class using mini-whiteboards, and by scanning or circulating the room. This provides the basis from which teachers adapt and respond, through their teaching, in the moment or subsequently. Examples include correcting students' answers, prompting them to self-correct, offering further explanation, exemplification or elaboration, or later on, adapting or planning lessons in light of the inferences they make. As a result, much formative assessment is not 'marked', but students receive continuous feedback through the everyday pedagogy of the history classroom.

> See chapters C1, D2 and D4.

Marking is usually associated with written work. If we use written answers for formative assessment in history, then we must read at least a sample of students' answers in order to be able to assess what students know and understand. We need to know this in order to inform our actions and/or feedback to students, to improve their knowledge and understanding. Similarly, if we set students another kind of outcome task in which they deliver a presentation, speech, podcast or video, for example, to demonstrate their knowledge and understanding, we would need to listen to these in order to assess their knowledge and understanding.

> See chapter D4. See also WalkThrus 1 Whole-class feedback and WalkThrus 2 Selective marking.

Reading or listening to a sample may, however, be sufficient for the purposes of formative assessment. Students in the same class who have attended the same lessons are likely to produce work of varying quality, but the strengths and weaknesses of their responses are likely to have much in common. A sample may therefore provide a sufficient basis for a history teacher to praise students on their common strengths, and to provide the formative feedback which moves students forward, for example using a whole-class feedback approach. A teacher may also identify some 'outliers' who require different feedback or follow-up actions.

Kate Hammond (2014) illustrated how teachers can make inferences from reading their students' work, or a selection of answers. Hammond attended closely to the language used by her students, and the way in which they deployed their knowledge about the topic, to make inferences about the kinds of knowledge students had or lacked, as well as the effect of this on the quality of their answers. There are examples of history teachers analysing their students' work to draw inferences about their learning, and acting on these, in the work of Ellis (2020), Jackson-Buckley and Phillips (2024), West and Longair (2023) and many other articles in the pages of *Teaching History*. Jonathan Grande (2024a) shared his approach, and how he records these inferences and uses them with his department in the evaluation and development of the curriculum, in a recent webinar series for the Historical Association.

Another similar approach is selective marking, where a teacher focuses on one particular section of students' work – the introduction, or a particular paragraph, or the conclusion – in order to provide targeted feedback on that area. This may be followed by an action such as redrafting.

While reading at least a sample of students' work is essential for teachers to make the inferences that will inform their teaching, this does not require written feedback, and certainly does not require the personalised written feedback to individuals generally associated with marking.

Marks and grades in formative assessment

Some kinds of formative assessment in history, such as a quiz, generate feedback in the form of right or wrong answers. Supplying the correct answers provides feedback to students on their knowledge which is both easy to understand and actionable: they can, independently or with guidance, revisit and revise questions they got wrong. Teachers can adapt their teaching to address areas of weakness in students' knowledge. Students can calculate their own score easily, or it may automatically be provided by a quiz undertaken on a digital platform.

See chapter D1.

Longer written answers in history, such as the outcome tasks used at the end of an enquiry, do not naturally generate feedback in the form of correct or incorrect answers. Teachers may provide feedback to students to correct factual errors or misunderstandings of substantive knowledge. It is not usually helpful to provide a score to students as part of their feedback on an extended written (or oral) answer. This is because students focus on a score or grade to the exclusion of attention to feedback. Students who received qualitative feedback without a quantitative score or grade made more progress, seemingly because they paid more attention to the qualitative feedback that showed them how to improve (Butler, 1988; Wiliam, 2011).

It may, however, be helpful for teachers to record a score alongside qualitative notes, as this can provide a useful shorthand record. If not used to inform a summative judgement, or shared, or compared with students in another class, these scores do not need to be standardised or moderated, or even to relate to standard criteria. This can reduce workload, while still ensuring that teachers have a record of meaningful information about their students, in the form of inferences from formative assessment.

Summative assessment

The purpose of summative assessment is, as explored in chapter D2, very different from that of formative assessment. While formative assessment is precisely targeted and

See chapter D2.

diagnostic, summative assessment is holistic. It samples broadly from the domain to support judgements about students' attainment and progress. Inferences from summative assessment inform evaluation and development of the curriculum. While formative assessment is useful for the class teacher and students, and to improve students' knowledge and understanding, the audience for summative assessment is largely outside the classroom: leaders and parents.

By its nature, the breadth of summative assessment means it is ill-suited to providing precise, usable feedback to students. It follows that marking, as traditionally understood, in the form of written comments on individual students' work, is unlikely to have sufficient impact to justify the time spent. Indeed, this is even less likely to be the case for summative assessment than for formative assessment.

Using descriptors or criteria to make judgements

To make a summative judgement about each student, however, teachers will need to read all their work, with the exception of those question types or assessment methods that can be automatically marked using digital platforms. Work is conventionally assessed using criteria, often called a mark scheme. Sally Burnham and Geraint Brown explored the use of mark schemes to assess written work in history in two seminal articles, published in 2004 and 2014.

Prior to 2014, national curriculum levels descriptions offered generic criteria against which to assess students' disciplinary knowledge in history at the end of Key Stage 3. Despite guidance to the contrary, these were routinely used by schools to assess individual pieces of work. Burnham and Brown advocated the use of task-specific mark schemes instead, devising criteria that combined the substantive and disciplinary knowledge. This offers a better assessment of students' historical knowledge and understanding, since doing history involves the integration of substantive with disciplinary knowledge. It offers more meaningful feedback to students and avoids the misleading characterisation of progression in history as a linear series of generic steps, or 'colouring by numbers' (Burnham and Brown, 2004). Burnham and Brown (2014) showed how this could be done without the need for a mark, grade or level to distract students from a focus on their feedback.

See chapter A1 and A2 for responses to national curriculum approaches to assessment, chapter A3 for substantive and disciplinary knowledge, and chapter A5.

In 2014, Burnham and Brown further developed their rationale for, and approach to, the use of enquiry questions and task-specific mark schemes for assessment in history. They characterised such mark schemes as 'professional tools to be used by teachers to judge progress and inform the feedback we give to pupils'. Burnham and Brown advocate the collaborative development of mark schemes as an exercise in professional development, both for specialist and non-specialist teachers of history. They show this approach ensures that assessment remains true to the discipline of history: to what a subject team wants students to learn and be able to do with the knowledge they have acquired by the end of an enquiry (Burnham and Brown, 2014).

Despite the widespread use of criteria in assessment, for example in the marking of GCSE and A-level examinations in history, criteria-based mark schemes present significant challenges. Christodoulou (2016) observes that 'making accurate judgements against [prose] descriptors feels as though it should be straightforward but, in actual fact, it leads to very significant difficulties because it is possible to interpret such statements in very different ways'. This leads to unreliable judgements, where teachers do not all assign the same score, grade or judgement to the same piece of work, despite using the same criteria or descriptors.

In the marking of examinations, this unreliability is addressed to some extent through standardisation training, in which exemplars are used to exemplify the standards required to meet certain criteria. This helps to standardise the interpretation of the criteria by different markers. This can also be done in school through standardisation and moderation.

> See chapter A2 for wider issues with GCSE assessment structures.

Using comparative methods to make judgements

Comparative judgement is an alternative to criteria-based marking that can be implemented in practice in school. Advocated by Christodoulou (2016), this involves ranking students' work through comparison and improves the reliability of assessment. Reliability is the extent to which different markers would award the same mark for the same answer. The reliability of marking is low in history at GCSE and A-level, meaning that markers often do not award the same mark to the same answer, or even the same grade (Ofqual, 2018).

Comparative judgement can be facilitated using online engines such as No More Marking. To arrive at a definitive rank order through comparative judgement, each piece of work must be read and judged against another multiple times. This is time-consuming to implement in practice and can have undesirable unintended consequences. For example, this method of assessment might lead a department to design assessments that generate only short answers, to speed up the process of judgement. It might compromise the reliability of the assessment if, in practice, markers only read the first paragraph of each answer, rather than reading the answer in full, in order to save time. In this situation, markers will not reliably assess the merits of each answer because they may not take account of the quality of knowledge or understanding shown later in the answer.

Additionally, altering the question design to suit comparative judgement might limit the validity of the assessment. Validity is the extent to which the assessment supports the inferences made from it about students' knowledge. To give an extreme example, a question asking students for the start and end date of the First World War would not be a valid assessment of their understanding of the causal factors contributing to it; even asking students to list causes or to select them in a multiple-choice question would not permit valid inferences about their understanding of causation or their ability to explain why the war broke out. Altering the question design to suit comparative judgement would limit the validity of the assessment because the question would not fully sample, and therefore students' answers would not fully represent, their knowledge and understanding of the curriculum.

> See *WalkThrus 3* Comparative judgement (pp. 78–9).
>
> For No More Marking, see: www.nomoremarking.com.
>
> On the reliability of exam grades, this blog by Dennis Sherwood discusses Ofqual's research paper: www.rethinkingassessment.com/rethinking-blogs/just-how-reliable-are-exam-grades.

A quicker alternative is to rank a sample of student responses using comparative judgement and then to use these as a set of exemplars against which to make judgements about the work of the remaining students in the cohort. Each exemplar answer can be assigned a mark, for example out of 10, and some exemplars might be awarded the same mark for different reasons. Teachers then read the work of the rest of the cohort and compare each student's work to the set of exemplars, deciding where they would place it within the rank order of the exemplars and assigning a mark accordingly.

This process compromises to an extent on reliability but remains more reliable than criteria-based mark schemes because it still requires teachers to make comparative judgements between examples of student work, rather than absolute judgements about a piece of work in relation to their interpretation of criteria or descriptors. By removing the need to make multiple judgements, it significantly reduces the time taken compared to a full comparative judgement process. This also reduces the perverse incentives that can affect reliability or validity.

Grading

School policies require history teachers and subject leaders to share data and report information about students' progress to leaders and parents in a wide variety of forms. Whether expressed as a word, a letter or a number, however, this frequently takes the form of a grade. Grades discretely categorise students into groups: A, B, C, or 9, 8, 7, or mastering, securing, developing, emerging. In reality, student performance is continuous, not discrete, and inferences about student performance and progress based on grades can be misleading (Christodoulou, 2016). It places the focus on certain students whose performance fell below an arbitrary threshold, and makes some small variations in performance appear significant, while others are overlooked.

Despite these drawbacks, grading cannot be avoided where this is required by school policies, and it has advantages for clarity of communication. Teachers and leaders of history therefore need to find ways to assign grades to students that are as meaningful as possible – and as unlikely as possible to mislead – to school leaders, parents and students. This is largely down to the methods used to design, administer and judge assessments. Raw scores generated by these processes can be converted to grades to fit with the school's policies.

Since there is no standardised curriculum or assessment at Key Stage 3 in history, assessment must be designed internally. There is usually no known relationship between outcomes on these internal assessments and outcomes on national tests such as GCSE examinations. Some MATs have attempted to establish a known relationship, but this is not currently realistic for most history departments (Davies, 2020). The use of standardised or scaled scores is therefore helpful to support the setting of grade boundaries, informed by the distribution of results, and to facilitate comparison of the performance of the same cohort on different assessments (Christodoulou, 2016, pp. 193–6).

Standardised scores remove the inevitable variability in difficulty between assessments. Where summative assessments are synoptic, these become more challenging as students progress through the curriculum and are tested on a sample of knowledge from a wider domain and on areas of the domain that they have studied less recently. Certain topics or types of analysis will also be inherently more challenging for students than others. Grade boundaries should therefore be set for each assessment. Where the same assessment is repeated for subsequent cohorts, retaining the same grade boundaries can enable comparison of the performance of different cohorts.

CHAPTER D4
FEEDBACK LOOPS

As we have seen in chapters D2 and D3, formative and summative feedback processes at different scales will, when used well, be integral to effective history teaching in practice. If students are to become increasingly independent over time, they will also need to receive timely feedback and to be supported in processes of checking, reviewing, and editing. Feedback loops at different scales help to clarify student knowledge, develop student independence, and drive iterative curriculum development.

> See WalkThrus 1 Feedback as actions and Feedback that moves forward.

Short-cycle feedback loops

As we have seen in chapter D2, short-cycle feedback loops are a crucial way to assess students' security in different kinds of knowledge, at different stages of the curriculum journey. In a particularly fertile application of this idea, Olivey has discussed the way in which carefully constructed sequences of formative questions can be used alongside class reading of an extended text to maximise attention and develop knowledge (Olivey, 2024). He describes using questions that check for listening during a whole-class reading. These include regular use of questions to check for foundational knowledge and using discussion techniques such as think, pair, share to ask questions that are designed to connect key ideas in the text together. Figure D4.1 gives examples of these integrative questions.

Questions spaced throughout a text on Thomas Paine and the American Revolution
What did Paine spend his time doing in Philadelphia?
What disturbed Paine about Britain's treatment of its American colonies?
How did Paine's pamphlet 'Common Sense' inspire other revolutionaries?

▲ Figure D4.1: Examples of integrative questions

The feedback loops generated by this questioning approach can help guard against misconceptions as well as consolidate knowledge, even during the reading of a single text.

These short-cycle feedback loops should be in action during other classroom activities as well. Teachers can continuously respond to students' thinking in a variety of ways. They might be sensitive to patterns of highlighting, placement or categorisation during a card sort or to the nature of paired discussions between students. As students' knowledge develops over time, additional feedback loops are needed. The example in the box that follows illustrates this in a more extended way.

> At the start of a lesson, Ms Carter asks her class to write a timeline of five key events in the reign of Tsar Nicholas II, drawing on their knowledge from four previous lessons addressing the enquiry question, 'Was Nicholas II the main cause of the October Revolution?' Students write these on mini-whiteboards, so that she can quickly gauge the knowledge of the whole class.
>
> Ms Carter notices that students recalled at least one of the 1905 Revolution and the revolution of February 1917. She also notices that the outbreak of the First World War is absent from the timelines drawn by most students. She knows that the events of the First World War are vital to understanding the additional pressure that was placed on Tsar Nicholas II and is also aware of the danger of confusion emerging around the multiple different revolutionary events in the unit.
>
> Ms Carter gives feedback to the class and makes careful decisions about what to address instantly and what to leave to future lessons. She decides to focus on reinforcing the chronological overview of events in Russia between 1900 and October 1917. This also allows her to draw clear distinctions between revolutions in response to the identified student misconceptions. Ms Carter also decides to touch on the First World War more lightly during this process but heavily emphasises its role in the following lesson when students begin to explore the relative importance of different causes of the October Revolution.
>
> By the end of the lesson, or the following lesson, students' knowledge of the key events and causes of the October Revolution has changed. Ms Carter checks this, targeting some individuals they identified during the lesson. The assessment has served its purpose but the 'data' it provided is now out of date.

Feedback on student work

As we saw in chapter D2, extended writing has a fundamental role in formative assessment in history, even though it can be difficult to use formatively. It will also be important for students to receive feedback on their written work in ways that support them to reflect, edit and improve over time. Individual written feedback has often been used to give feedback on extended writing, but this has been shown to be an ineffective use of teacher time (Education Endowment Foundation, 2021). Instead, whole-class feedback approaches offer the possibility of supporting meaningful reflection among students while taking much less time. This approach can be married with giving students clearly specified action tasks to support their application of the feedback (Sherrington, 2017).

> See chapter C5 on writing and WalkThrus 1 Whole-class feedback.

To avoid genericism, it is vital to keep the history at the heart of the writing and therefore the feedback process. Writing should be embraced as an iterative process and intentionally incorporate subject-sensitive deliberate practice. Paula Worth used features of scholarship to exemplify the specific features of effective introductions in history essays (Worth, 2016). She used the metaphor of a seashell to demonstrate that an effective introduction in history must begin with its central claim before spiralling outwards into the rest of its argument. One way to approach this is to share common areas of success and for development, and to exemplify these with models. These might be responses by current or past students, or teacher-written models. Models play an important role in the process because they help make the areas of development concrete and therefore more easily actionable as well as ensure that the feedback process remains rooted in the subject and the topic and does not become meaninglessly generic. It is also crucial that students are asked to think, reflect and apply feedback so that they think deeply about it. Figure D4.2 illustrates how a whole-class feedback sequence might work for an A-level essay focused on how successfully Elizabeth I used her gender to enhance her power.

Step	Explanation
1. Scan and identify patterns	The teacher reads the class essays, and notes areas of strength and potential areas for development as they read.
2. Decide on a specific focus	The teacher identifies the conclusions to the essays as needing particular attention. They often fall back on simplistic explanation and do not adequately consider the whole of Elizabeth I's reign.
3. Write/extract models	The teacher turns to Diana Laffin's work on the habits of thinking and writing that historians demonstrate (Laffin, 2013). Laffin writes that historians are 'interested in time' and suggests language that the teacher thinks would be useful to the students. The teacher then writes two model conclusions. One conclusion exemplifies the problems that their students encountered and the second conclusion integrates Laffin's way of thinking about time to consider how Elizabeth I's gender was a great strength earlier in her reign and became more of a problem, 1588–1603 when marriage and an heir was no longer possible.
4. Exploration of models in class	The teacher then reads both model conclusions with the class under a visualiser. The students are asked to list the differences between the first and second model conclusion on mini-whiteboards.
5. Redrafting	Students redraft the conclusion to their essays, incorporating the idea of being 'interested in time' as well as the language that was used in the second model conclusion. In a supported reflection, students identify and highlight the language that shows they are 'interested in time' in their judgement.

▲ Figure D4.2: A possible feedback sequence for an A-level essay

Curricular feedback loops

Feedback loops, at a range of scales, are also integral to the iterative process of curriculum evaluation and development. Teachers make multiple micro-curricular decisions about emphasis, detail and sequencing in each lesson and across each enquiry. These decisions are challenging to make. Reflecting on these, informed by continuous assessment, allows teachers to improve their day-to-day practice and the implementation of the curriculum. Many teachers will be familiar with the experience of teaching a lesson for the second time, or the second year, and finding it goes more smoothly, informed by their earlier experience.

The kinds of data that are captured through these feedback loops are not likely to be quantitative, nor the kind of data that informs reports to senior leaders or parents about the progress of individual students or of a class or cohort. Instead, the data captured in this way is likely to be qualitative and most useful for reflection and discussion by individual teachers and department teams, informing future curriculum planning and teaching, both for the current cohort and for future cohorts. [See chapter D2.]

This kind of feedback loop works at a range of scales. A teacher might replan a lesson or the next lesson to address an immediate issue. A department might decide to resequence a unit, or even the whole curriculum, in response to emergent issues. Time dedicated by subject leaders for shared curricular reflection and evolution, as a part of departmental professional development planning, is invaluable for maximising the impact of curricular feedback loops.

APPENDIX 1

From a document produced by Hugh Richards, Huntington School, York, in collaboration with Richard Kennett, Redland Green School, Bristol. The document is given to pupils, but also used by staff as a reference point. It outlines core knowledge takeaways.

Living under Nazi Rule: Germany from democracy to dictatorship, 1933–34.

Nazi ideology promised a mighty and aggressive Germany

- Nazis believed that Germany should ignore the harsh restrictions placed on it by the Allies after WW1.
- With the economy in crisis, the Nazis promised **'Bread and Work'** for all.
- Nazis also wanted to ensure **Aryan** superiority and crush other peoples like **Jews** and political groups like **communists**.
- Nazis wanted to take large parts of Eastern Europe by force. This was called **lebensraum**.
- Nazis wanted more power and a strong government.

The Reichstag Fire led to Hitler removing the communists

- In February 1933 the Reichstag building burned down.
- Marinus Van der Lubbe, a Dutch communist, was arrested, convicted and sentenced to death.
- Hitler used the event to persuade Hindenburg to pass the Reichstag Fire Decree.
- The decree immediately limited the rights of a citizen when under arrest, freedom of expression, the right to public assembly and established harsher punishments for certain crimes.
- More than 4000 communists were arrested as a result.
- The Nazis used the decree to get rid of many important communist MPs, candidates and voters before the elections in March.

The Enabling Act made Hitler dictator of Germany

- SA stormtroopers intimidated other parties and voters in the build-up to the 1933 election.
- After the election, the Nazis formed a coalition with DNVP allowing them to pass any laws.
- Within weeks, Hitler passed the Enabling Act – this allowed Hitler to pass any law without consent of the Reichstag.
- It made Hitler dictator of Germany.

Gleichschaltung created a culture of fear and oppression

- Gleichschaltung means bringing Germany into line.
- The Civil Service Act (February 1933) meant Nazi-opponents and non-Aryans were sacked in professions like teaching and law.
- In March 1933 the first concentration camp was set up at Dachau leading to a reign of terror.
- In April 1933 the Nazis organized a day-long boycott of Jewish businesses.
- In May 1933 Goebbels encouraged Nazi student groups to burn 'un-German' books

APPENDIX 2

'Curriculum design: questions to support analysis and evaluation' – handout for trainee teachers, compiled by Geraint Brown

Questions about the scope of the curriculum

- What is the balance between British, European and world history? Local, national, international?
- What is the chronological spread of the curriculum?
- Does the curriculum reflect the diversity of your student body or of Britain in terms of race, gender, class, etc.? How far should it? How far does it/should it respond to current issues and affairs in the world?
- Whose voices are being heard? Whose narrative, or what type of narrative, is reflected in the curriculum? Is the curriculum too Whiggish, too white, too British, too…?
- What is *not* taught and why? Are particular aspects of world history ignored?
- Does local history feature and how is this used to support and strengthen the curriculum?
- Is there 'scale-switching' (e.g. from breadth to depth) to help pupils situate particular events in a broader framework or narrative?

Questions about the sequence of the curriculum

- What is the rationale for the order of the topics and enquiries?
- Is the rationale for the sequence rooted in both the substantive and disciplinary knowledge?
- What is the purpose and function of *this* part of the curriculum *here*? Why *this*, why *now*?
- What secure foundations of knowledge do pupils need [by the end of Y7, 8 , 9] that will act as a useful base on which to build later on [at GCSE/A-Level]? How does this enquiry in [Y8] support pupils' thinking in [Y10]?

- What 'fingertip' and/or 'residue' knowledge' will pupils need to navigate through this part of the curriculum or make sense of the next part of the narrative?
- What do pupils need to retain from one enquiry/year to the next?
- *How* does knowledge of prior periods *enable* and *assist* knowledge of later periods.

Questions about the coherence of the curriculum

- What substantive concepts do pupils develop knowledge and understanding of over time?
- Do substantive concepts such as 'power', 'religion', 'people', 'empire', 'revolution' and 'trade' occur – and recur – throughout the curriculum?
- What specific factual knowledge do pupils need to gain or retain in one year so it can be manifested and operate and enable them to succeed in the next?
- What knowledge will pupils gain to be able to make meaningful comparisons across time and place?
- How do the types of questions that pupils ask and answer, or units they study, have resonance across the key stages?
- How is pupils' developing knowledge helping them build chronological frameworks?
- Are there overarching questions or themes that are returned to help make links across the curriculum and join things together? What other strategies help to achieve this?

Questions about the rigour of the curriculum

- Are the questions pupils are being asked to address, or units they are engaged in, increasing in challenge, enabling them to make progress in the discipline as well as in their substantive knowledge?
- Is the Year 8 course actually more difficult than the Year 7 course? Is this about detail, depth, complexity, independence, pace, the question, the concept...
- Does the curriculum reflect a clear understanding of what progress looks like in history?
- What does it mean to get better at [causal reasoning] and how is this manifested in the type of question asked and specific topic being studied?

- Are the topics/enquiry questions grounded in and reflecting the [recent] scholarship of historians?
- Has the department 'wrestled' with the wording of the enquiry question and carefully 'chosen and planted' them across the key stage?
- How might you assess pupils' cumulative acquisition of knowledge, their changing knowledge & understanding of substantive concepts and their ability to use knowledge to think historically?

BIBLIOGRAPHY

AQA (2021) *Teaching guide: AO4 questions - AQA*. filestore.aqa.org.uk/resources/history/AQA-8145-TG-AO4.PDF.

Ashbee, R. (2021) *Curriculum: Theory, Culture and the Subject Specialisms*. Routledge.

Bailey-Watson, W. (2019) 'To think that these things did actually happen...: structuring a history curriculum for powerful revelations', *Teaching History* 174, pp. 53–61.

Bailey-Watson, W. and Kennett, R. (2019) "Meanwhile, elsewhere...': harnessing the power of community to expand students' historical horizons', *Teaching History* 176, pp. 36–43.

Bateman, C. (2018) "I need to know...': creating the conditions that make students want knowledge', *Teaching History* 173, pp. 32–39.

Beck, I., McKeown, M. G. and Kucan, L. (2013) *Bringing Words to Life: Robust Vocabulary Instruction*. The Guilford Press.

Bridges, A. (2018) 'The particular and the general: defining security in Year 8's use of substantive concepts', *Teaching History* 171, pp. 56–65.

Brown, G. and Burnham, S. (2004) 'Assessment without level descriptions', *Teaching History* 115, pp. 5–15.

Brown, G. and Burnham, S. (2014) 'Assessment after levels', *Teaching History* 157, pp. 8–17.

Brown, G., Fordham, M. and Stanford, M. (2012) 'Triumphs Show: Professional wrestling in department meetings', *Teaching History* 146, pp. 8–17.

Butler, R. (1988) 'Enhancing and undermining intrinsic motivation: the effects of task-involving and ego-involving evaluation on interest and performance', *British Journal of Educational Psychology* 58, pp. 1–14.

Byrom, J. and Riley, M. (2003) 'Professional wrestling in the history department: a case study in planning the teaching of the British Empire at Key Stage 3', *Teaching History* 112, pp. 6–14.

Cannadine, D., Keating, J. and Sheldon, N. (2011) *The Right Kind of History: Teaching the Past in Twentieth-Century England*. Palgrave Macmillan.

Card, J. (2004) 'Seeing double: how one period visualises another', *Teaching History* 117, pp. 6–11.

Carr, E. (2021) 'Power, authority and geography: medieval political history through the stories of powerful women', *Teaching History* 184, pp. 70–80.

Carr, E. and Counsell, C. (2014) 'Using time-lines in assessment', *Teaching History* 157, pp. 54–62.

Carroll, J. (2016) 'The whole point of the thing: how nominalisation might develop students' written causal arguments', *Teaching History* 162, pp. 16–25.

Carroll, J. (2017) '"I feel if I say this in my essay it's not going to be as strong': multi-voicedness, 'oral rehearsal' and Year 13 students' written arguments', *Teaching History* 167, pp. 8–16.

Carroll, J. (2018a) 'Couching counterfactuals in knowledge when explaining the Salem witch trials with Year 13', *Teaching History* 172, pp. 18–29.

Carroll, J. (2018b) 'Duplo to watercolours: how the substantive might shape the disciplinary in students' historical causal arguments'. J Carroll History [blog] 2 March. www.jcarrollhistory.com/2018/03/02/duplo-to-watercolours-how-the-substantive-might-shape-the-disciplinary-in-students-causal-arguments/.

Carroll, J. (2022) 'Terms and conditions: using metaphor to highlight causal processes with Year 13', *Teaching History* 187, pp. 40–49.

Chapman, A. (2011) 'Understanding historical knowing: evidence and accounts', in Perikleous, L. and Shemilt, D. (eds), *The Future of the Past*, Association for Historical Dialogue and Research, pp. 169–214.

Christodoulou, D. (2017) *Making Good Progress? The Future of Assessment for Learning*. Oxford University Press.

Counsell, C. (2003) 'Who cares about Charles I? Cunning plan for a lesson on C.V. Wedgwood's writing', *Teaching History* 111, p. 37.

Counsell, C. (2004) *History and Literacy in Year 7: Building the lesson around the text*. Hodder Education.

Counsell, C. (2011) 'Historical knowledge and historical skills: a distracting dichotomy', in Arthur, J. and Phillips, R. (eds) *Issues in History Teaching*, Routledge, pp. 54–71.

Counsell, C. (2017) 'The fertility of substantive knowledge: in search of its hidden, generative power', in Davies, I. (ed) *Debates in History Teaching* (2nd ed), Routledge, pp. 80–99.

Counsell, C. (2018a) 'Senior Curriculum Leadership 1: The indirect manifestation of knowledge: (A) curriculum as narrative'. The Dignity of the Thing [blog] 7 April. www.thedignityofthethingblog. wordpress.com/2018/04/07/senior-curriculum-leadership-1-the-indirect-manifestation-of-knowledge-a-curriculum-as-narrative/.

Counsell, C. (2018b) 'Taking curriculum seriously', *Impact* 4.

Counsell, C. (2023) 'Laughing muppets, lost memories and lethal mutations: rescuing assessment from 'knowledge-rich gone wrong'', *Teaching History* 193, pp. 8–25.

Counsell, C., et al. (2024) *Connected Worlds, c.1000–c.1600*. Hodder Education.

Culpin, C. (2002) 'Why we must change history GCSE', *Teaching History* 109, pp. 6–9.

Culpin, C. (2007) 'The 2007 Medlicott Medal Lecture: What kind of history should school history be?'. Historical Association [Online] 31 August. www.history.org.uk/historian/resource/747/the-2007-medlicott-medal-lecture-what-kind-of-hist.

Cusworth, H. (2021) 'Putting black into the Union Jack: weaving Black history into the Year 7 to 9 curriculum', *Teaching History* 183, pp. 20–26.

Davies, R. (2020) 'Strength in numbers: operationalising a network-wide assessment model', in Donarski, S. (ed) *The ResearchEd Guide to Assessment*, John Catt, pp. 78–89.

Dawson, I. (2008) 'Thinking across time: planning and teaching the story of power and democracy at Key Stage 3', *Teaching History* 130, pp. 14–23.

Dawson, I. (ed) (2018) *Exploring and Teaching Medieval History in Schools*. Historical Association.

Dawson, I. (n.d.) 'The Nature and Significance of Enquiry in History Teaching'. Thinking History [blog]. www.thinkinghistory.co.uk/EnquirySkill/EnquiryImportance.html.

Dennis, N. (2017) 'Beyond tokenism: teaching a diverse history in the post-14 curriculum', *Teaching History* 165, pp. 37–41.

Department of Education and Science (1985) *History in the primary and secondary years: an HMI view*. HMSO.

Department of Education and Science (1988) *History 5–16 – Curriculum Matters 11, An HMI Series*. HMSO.

Department of Education and Science (1989) *Interim Report of the History Working Group*. DES & the Welsh Office.

Department of Education and Science (1990) *Final Report of the History Working Group*. DES & the Welsh Office.

Department of Education and Science (1990) *History in the National Curriculum (England)*. HMSO.

Department of Education and Science (1991) *History in the National Curriculum (England)*. HMSO.

Department for Education (2013) *National curriculum in England: history programmes of study*. www.gov.uk/government/publications/national-curriculum-in-england-history-programmes-of-study/national-curriculum-in-england-history-programmes-of-study.

Department for Education (2014) *History programmes of study: Key Stage 3*. https://assets.publishing.service.gov.uk/government/uploads/system/uploads/attachment_data/file/239075/SECONDARY_national_curriculum_-_History.pdf.

Dickson, A. (2017) 'Managing the scope of study: is it as easy as Key Stage 3', *Teaching History* 168, pp. 37–45.

Dunn, R. E. (2008) 'The Two World Histories', *Social Education*, 72(5), pp. 257–263.

Durbin, E. (2018) '"Its ultimate pattern was greater than its parts": using a patchwork quilt analogy at Key Stage 3 to support analytical thinking at GCSE', *Teaching History* 180, pp. 8–15.

Education Endowment Foundation (2020) *Metacognition and self-regulated learning guidance report*. https://educationendowmentfoundation.org.uk/education-evidence/guidance-reports/metacognition.

Education Endowment Foundation (2021) *Teacher feedback to improve pupil learning guidance report*. https://educationendowmentfoundation.org.uk/education-evidence/guidance-reports/feedback.

Ellis, J. (2020) 'What's in a narrative? Unpicking Year 9 narratives of change in Stalin's Russia', *Teaching History* 178, pp. 32–41.

Evans, R. (1997) *In Defence of History*. Granta Books.

Evans, J. and Pate, G. (2007) 'Does scaffolding make them fall? Reflecting on strategies for developing causal argument in Years 8 and 11', *Teaching History* 128, pp. 18–29.

Ford, A. (2019) 'Visions of America: using historical discourse to find narrative coherence in the GCSE period study', *Teaching History* 176, pp. 10–21.

Fordham, M. (2007) 'Slaying dragons and sorcerers in Year 12: in search of historical argument', *Teaching History* 129, pp. 31–38.

Fordham, M. (2014) 'Are we training pupils to be historians?'. *Clio et cetera* [blog] 20 March. www.clioetcetera.com/2014/03/20/are-we-training-pupils-to-be-historians.

Fordham, M. (2014) '"But why then?' Chronological context and historical interpretations', *Teaching History* 156, pp. 32–39.

Fordham, M. (2017a) 'Substantive concepts at KS2 & KS3'. *Clio et cetera* [blog] 9 November. www.clioetcetera.com/2017/11/09/substantive-concepts-at-ks2-ks3/.

Fordham, M. (2017b) 'Solving the history textbook conundrum: a five-point manifesto'. Clio et cetera [blog] 15 December. www.clioetcetera.com/2017/12/15/solving-the-history-textbook-conundrum-a-five-point-manifesto.

Fordham, M. (2017c) 'Decoupling summative and formative assessment'. Clio et cetera [blog] 2 November. www.clioetcetera.com/2017/11/02/decoupling-summative-and-formative-assessment.

Fordham, M. (2017d) 'Assessment', in Davies, I. (ed) *Debates in History Teaching, Second Edition*, Routledge, pp. 284–294.

Fordham, M. (2020) 'What did I mean by 'the curriculum is the progression model'?'. Clio et ceterea [blog] 8 February. www.clioetcetera.com/2020/02/08/what-did-i-mean-by-the-curriculum-is-the-progression-model.

Foster, R. (2011) 'Passive receivers or constructive readers? Pupils' experiences of an encounter with academic history', *Teaching History* 142, pp. 4-13.

Foster, R. (2014) 'The more things change, the more they stay the same: developing students' thinking about change and continuity', *Teaching History* 151, pp. 8–17.

Foster, R. and Goudie, K. (2019) 'A b c d e? Teaching Year 9 to take on the challenge of structure in narrative', *Teaching History* 175, pp. 28–39.

Frankopan, P. (2018) *The Silk Roads: The Extraordinary History that created your World*. Bloomsbury.

Grande, J. (2022) 'This week in history... why the hinterland is core'. Curricular pasts: reflections from a history classroom [online] 6 March. www.curricularpasts.wordpress.com/2022/03/06/6-this-week-in-history-why-the-hinterland-is-core/.

Grande, J. (2023) 'Why I teach pupils things I don't need them to remember for ever: the role of takeaways in shaping a history curriculum', *Teaching History* 192, pp. 18–29.

Grande, J. (2024a) 'More than remembering: stories, knowledge and assessment', Ark Soane History Conference, 3rd February 2024.

Grande, J. (2024b) 'Assessment in History' webinar series. Historical Association.

Guyver, R. (2013) 'Landmarks with questions – England's school history wars 1967–2010 and 2010–2013', *History Education Research Journal*, 11(2), pp. 59–87.

Hammond, K. (2014) 'The knowledge that 'flavours' a claim: towards building and assessing historical knowledge on three scales', *Teaching History* 157, pp. 18–24.

Hawkey, K. (2023) *History and the Climate Crisis: Environmental history in the classroom*. UCL Press, p. 8.

Hawkey, K., et al. (2024) 'History and the climate crisis: Bristol history teachers explore environmental history in the classroom', *Teaching History* 194, pp. 13–21.

Head, S. (2020) '"That's just the tip of the iceberg': building Key Stage 5 students' analysis of interpretations in the short, medium and long term', *Teaching History* 180, pp. 57–63.

Hesseltine, W. B. (1945) 'The Challenge of the Civil War', *Mississippi Valley Historical Review*, 32(3), p. 331.

Hibbert, D. and Patel, Z. (2019) 'Modelling the discipline: how can Yasmin Khan's use of evidence enable us to teach a more global World War II?', *Teaching History* 177, pp. 8–15.

Hill, M. (2020) 'Curating the imagined past: world building in the history curriculum', *Teaching History* 180, pp. 10–20.

Hill, M. (2023) 'Forms and meanings: how can we teach abstract words in the history classroom?', presentation at TeachMeet History Icons, Chelmsford, October 2023.

Hirsch, E. D. (2016) *Why Knowledge Matters: rescuing our children from failed educational theories*. Harvard Educational Press.

Historical Association (2003) 'Nutshell', *Teaching History* 113, p. 48.

Historical Association (2008) 'The National Curriculum Attainment Target (from 2008)'. www.history.org.uk/secondary/categories/639/resource/2127/the-national-curriculum-attainment-target-from-20.

Historical Association (2019) 'What's the wisdom on... Interpretations of the past', *Teaching History 177*, pp. 23–7.

Historical Association (2020) 'What's the wisdom on... enquiry questions?', *Teaching History 185*, pp. 16–19.

Historical Association (2021a) 'What's the wisdom on... history assessment?', *Teaching History 185*, pp. 56–59.

Historical Association (2021b) 'What's the wisdom on... extended reading?', *Teaching History 183*, pp. 44–47.

Jackson-Buckley, S. and Phillips, J. (2024) 'Disembarking the religious rollercoaster: a new 'direction' for studying the consequences of the Reformation', *Teaching History 195*, pp. 6-16.

Jenkins, K. (1991) *Re-thinking History*. Routledge.

Jenner, T. (2019) 'Making reading routine: helping Key Stage 3 pupils to become regular readers of historical scholarship', *Teaching History 174*, pp. 42–48.

Kaufmann, M. (2017) *Black Tudors: The Untold Story*. Oneworld.

Kerridge, R. (2017) 'Learning without limits: how not to leave some learners with a thin gruel of a curriculum', *Teaching History 168*, pp. 16–22.

Kesterton, N. (2019) 'Using narratives and big pictures to address the challenges of a 2-year KS3 curriculum,' *Teaching History 176*, pp. 26–33.

Lacey, G. and Shepherd, K. (1997) *Germany 1918–1945*. Hodder Education.

Laffin, D. (2013) 'Marr: Magpie or Marsh Harrier? The quest for the common characteristics of the genus 'historian' with 16- to 19-year-olds', *Teaching History 149*, pp. 18–25.

Lang, S. (2003) 'Narrative: the underrated skill', *Teaching History 110*, pp. 8–17.

Lee, P., Ashby, R. and Dickinson, A. (1993) 'Progression in Children's Ideas about History. Project CHATA (Concepts of History and Teaching Approaches: 7 to 14)'. Paper presented at the Annual Meeting of the British Educational Research Association (Liverpool, England, September 11).

Lee, P. (1998) ''A lot of guess work goes on': children's understanding of historical accounts', *Teaching History 92*, pp. 29–35.

Lee, P. (2017) 'History education and historical literacy', in Davies, I. (ed) *Debates in History Teaching* (2nd edition), Routledge, pp. 55–65.

Lemov, D. (2017) 'Why reading aloud to students is so critical to vocabulary'. Teach Like A Champion [blog] 25 April. www.teachlikeachampion.org/blog/reading-aloud-students-critical-vocabulary.

Lemov, D. (2021) *Teach like a Champion 3.0*. Jossey-Bass.

Lewin, R. (2022) 'Interdisciplinarity with integrity', in Fairlamb, A. and Ball, R. (eds) *What is History Teaching, Now? A practical handbook for all history teachers and educators*, John Catt, p. 220.

Lewin, R. (2023) 'Migration', in Ball, R. and Fairlamb, A. (eds) *What is History Teaching, Now? A practical handbook for all history teachers and educators*, John Catt, p. 398.

Luff, I. (2000) 'I've been in the Reichstag: re-thinking role play', *Teaching History* 100, pp. 8–17.

Luff, I. (2001) 'Beyond 'I speak you listen, boy!' Exploring diversity of attitudes and experiences through speaking and listening', *Teaching History* 105, pp. 10–18.

Luff, I. (2003) 'Stretching the strait jacket of assessment: use of role play and PD to enrich pupils' experience of history at GCSE and beyond', *Teaching History* 113, pp. 26–35.

Luff, I. (2023) 'Practical demonstration: powerful and rigorous history teaching for all', *Teaching History* 191, pp. 30–42.

Lydon-Cohen, D. (2006) 'Integrating black British history into the National Curriculum', *Teaching History* 122, pp. 37–43.

Lydon-Cohen, D. (2021) 'Decolonise, don't diversify: enabling a paradigm shift in the Key Stage 3 history curriculum', *Teaching History* 183, pp. 50–57.

Macintosh, H. G. (1979) 'The Schools Council History 13-16 Project The CSE Examination Some Problems of Assessment: Part One', *Teaching History* 24, pp. 22–25.

Manning, P. (2003) *Navigating World History: historians create a global past*. Palgrave Macmillan.

McAleavy, T. (1993) 'Using the Attainment Targets in Key Stage 3: AT2, 'Interpretations of History', *Teaching History* 72, pp. 14–17.

McAleavy, T. (1998) 'The use of sources in school history 1910–1998: a critical perspective', *Teaching History* 91, pp. 10–16.

McCrory, C. (2015) 'The knowledge illusion', *Teaching History* 161, pp. 37–47.

Mohamud, A. and Whitburn, R. (2016) *Doing Justice to History: transforming Black history in secondary schools*. Trentham Books.

Moorhouse, D. (2009) 'How to make historical simulations adaptable, engaging and manageable', *Teaching History* 133, pp. 10–16.

Morton, T. and Seixas, P. (2013) *The Big Six Historical Thinking Concepts*. Nelson.

Myatt, M. and Tomsett, J. (2021) *Huh: curriculum conversations between subject and senior leaders*. John Catt, pp. 163–76.

Nordgren, K. (2021) 'Powerful knowledge for what? History education and 45-degree discourse', in Chapman, A. (ed) *Knowing History in Schools: powerful knowledge and the powers of knowledge*, UCL Press, p. 177–202.

OCR (2023) *Specification history A*. www.ocr.org.uk/Images/207163-specification-accredited-gcse-history-a-first-teaching-2019-with-first-assessment-2021-j410.pdf.

OCR (2023) *Specification history B*. www.ocr.org.uk/Images/207164-specification-accredited-gcse-history-b-.pdf.

Ofqual (2018) 'Marking consistency metrics – an update'. https://assets.publishing.service.gov.uk/government/uploads/system/uploads/attachment_data/file/759207/Marking_consistency_metrics_-_an_update_-_FINAL64492.pdf.

Ofsted (2007) *History in the balance: history in English schools 2003–07*. www.dera.ioe.ac.uk/id/eprint/7089/1/History_in_the_balance_(PDF_format).pdf.

Ofsted (2011) *History for all: history in English schools 2007/10*. www.gov.uk/government/publications/history-for-all-strengthes-and-weaknesses-of-school-history-teaching.

Ofsted (2021) *Research review series: history*. www.gov.uk/government/publications/research-review-series-history.

Ofsted (2023) *Rich encounters with the past: history subject report*. www.gov.uk/government/publications/subject-report-series-history/rich-encounters-with-the-past-history-subject-report.

Olivey, J. (2021) 'They sometimes clashed, and ultimately blended: planning a more diverse and coherent Year 7 curriculum', *Teaching History* 184, pp. 22–31.

Olivey, J. (2024) 'One Story, One Lesson: how to write and teach a story summary', Ark Soane History Conference, 3rd February 2024.

Olusoga, D. (2016) *Black and British: A Forgotten History*. Macmillan.

Palek, D. (2015) '"What exactly is parliament?" Finding the place of substantive knowledge in history', *Teaching History* 158, pp. 18–25.

Paxon, R. J. (1999) 'A deafening silence: history textbooks and the students who read them', *Review of Educational Research*, 69(3), pp. 315–339.

Pearson Edexcel (2016) Guidance on sources and interpretations – Pearson qualifications. https://qualifications.pearson.com/content/dam/

pdf/GCSE/History/2016/Teaching-and-learning-materials/GCSE_History_Sources_and_interpretations_guide.pdf.

Priggs, C. (2020) 'No more 'doing' diversity: how one department used Year 8 input to reform curricular thinking about content choice', *Teaching History* 179, pp. 10–19.

Quigley, A. (2020) *Closing the Reading Gap*. Routledge.

Quigley, A. (2022) *Closing the Writing Gap*. Routledge.

Richards, H. (2019) 'Ringing the changes: the power of enquiry questions that both chime and resonate'. Historical Association: One Big History Department, 12 July. www.onebighistorydepartment.com/2019/07/12/ringing-the-changes-the-power-of-enquiry-questions-that-both-chime-and-resonate.

Richards, H. (2021) 'Making thinking visible in History', in Tomsett, J. (ed) *Cognitive Apprenticeship in Action*, John Catt, pp. 29–36.

Richards, R. (2023) 'Corners of foreign fields: ideas for making meaning and memory on a Battlefields Trip'. Historical Association [blog] 17 May. www.onebighistorydepartment.com/2023/05/17/corners-of-foreign-fields-ideas-for-making-meaning-and-memory-on-a-battlefields-trips.

Richardson, H. (2000) 'The QCA history scheme of work for Key Stage 3', *Teaching History* 99, pp. 14–9.

Riley, M. (2000) 'Into the Key Stage 3 history garden: choosing and planting your enquiry questions', *Teaching History* 99, pp. 8–13.

Rosenshine, B. (2012) 'Principles of Instruction: Research-Based Strategies that All Teachers Should Know', *American Educator*, Spring, pp. 12–39.

Royal Historical Society (2018) 'Race, Ethnicity & Equality in UK History: a report and resource for change'. www.royalhistsoc.org/racereport/.

Scott, J. (ed) (1990) *Understanding Cause and Effect: learning and teaching about causation and consequence in History* (Teaching History Research Group). Longman.

Sellin, J. (2018) 'Trampolines and Springboards: exploring the fragility of 'source and own knowledge' with Year 10', *Teaching History* 171, pp. 32–39.

Sherrington, T. (2017) '#FiveWays of Giving Effective Feedback as Actions'. Teacherhead [blog] 18 December. www.teacherhead.com/2017/12/18/fiveways-of-giving-effective-feedback-as-actions.

Sherrington, T. (2023) 'Genericism and Specialism in Teacher Development: ideals and realities'. Teacherhead [blog] 14 March. www.teacherhead.

171

com/2023/03/14/genericism-and-specialism-in-teacher-development-ideals-and-realities/.

Sherrington, T. and Caviglioli, O. (2020) *Teaching WalkThrus: five-step guides for instructional coaching*. John Catt.

Spafford, M. (2023) 'How should young people "feel" and "do" history? How may this shape their world?', Dawson Lecture, Historical Association Annual Conference.

Stanford, M. (2019) 'Did the Bretons break? Planning increasingly complex causal models at Key Stage 3', *Teaching History* 175, pp. 8–15.

Tosh, J. (2022) *The Pursuit of History: Aims, Methods and New Directions in the Study of History*. Routledge.

Traille, K. (2007) '"You should be proud about your history. They made me feel ashamed": teaching history hurts', *Teaching History* 127, pp. 31–37.

Vallance, J. (2021) 'Core and hinterland: what are we really talking about?'. Mr Vallance Teach [blog] 15 May. www.mrvallanceteach.wordpress.com/2021/05/15/core-and-hinterland-what-are-we-really-talking-about.

West, G. and Longair, S. (2023) ''But they just sit there': using objects as material culture with Year 8', *Teaching History* 191, pp. 44–52.

Whitburn, R. and Yemoh, S. (2012) ''My people struggled too': hidden histories and heroism – a school-designed, post-14 course on multi-cultural Britain since 1945', *Teaching History* 147, pp. 16–25.

Wiliam, D. (2011) *Embedded Formative Assessment*. Solution Tree Press, pp. 107–113.

Willingham, D. T. (2009) *Why Don't Students Like School? A cognitive scientist answers questions about how the mind works and what it means for your classroom*. Jossey-Bass.

Wineburg, S. (2001) *Historical Thinking and Other Unnatural Acts: charting the future of teaching the past*. Temple University Press.

Woodcock, J. (2005) 'Does the linguistic release the conceptual? Helping Year 10 to improve their causal reasoning', *Teaching History* 119, pp. 5–23.

Woolley, M. (2003) '"Really weird and freaky": using a Thomas Hardy short story as a source of evidence in the Year 8 classroom', *Teaching History* 111, pp. 6–11.

Worth, P. (2014) '"English King Frederick I won at Arsuf, then took Acre, then they all went home": exploring the challenges involved in reading and writing historical narrative', *Teaching History* 156, pp. 8–19.

Worth, P. (2016) '"My initial concern is to get a hearing": exploring what makes an effective history essay introduction', *Teaching History* 164, pp. 10–21.

Worth, P. (2018) 'Here ends the lesson: shaping lesson conclusions', *Teaching History* 173, pp. 58–67.

Worth, P. (2023) 'Falling forward: three strategies to support pupils' study of historical significance', *Teaching History* 190, pp. 8–21.

Wrenn, A., et al. (2013) 'Teaching Emotive and Controversial History 3-19'. Historical Association. https://www.history.org.uk/secondary/categories/487/module/1140/teach-online.

Yale Nicholson, P. (2004) *Labor's Story in the United States*. Temple University Press.

Zinn, H. (1999) *A People's History of the United States*. HarperCollins.